"Many well-meaning Christians believe the God of Islam is the same as the God of Christianity. *Who is this Allah?* answers this problem. It meets a great need."
—   B. Trevor, Australia

"I fasted for some years that God would show me the true religion (Islam or Christianity)... Thank you very much for writing this book. God has shown me the true way."
—   B. Ibrahim

"*Who is this Allah?* is logical and should appeal to all Muslims. Wonderful!"
—   Sir Lionel Luckhoo
Honored four times by Queen Elizabeth II

"This book has really helped us to better understand Islam and how to approach Muslims with the Gospel."
—   P.L. Mendy, Missionary in the Gambia

"*Who is this Allah?* burns with vitality, sincerity, courage, sacrifice and intellectual honesty about Islam."
—   A pastor in Midlands, UK

"... the most exciting literature on this subject that I have come across."
—   C. Kamanga, University of Reading, UK

"A model for believers who want to witness to Muslims. Gentle, but unflinchingly firm."
—   *The Berean Call,* Christian Newsletter

"... answers many of the common questions that form barriers keeping Muslims from the Gospel."
— *Battle Cry,* Christian Newsletter

"...an excellent book, most readable and very cogent and convincing..."
— William Penfold, UK

"I have never received such a great number of requests for a book."
> – Editor, *Global Prayer Digest of U.S. Center for World Mission*

"*Who is this Allah?* stands out prominently as a clear distinct message of the Lord Jesus Christ."
> – O.K., Tathleeth, Saudi Arabia.

"… a timely and significant book. Essential reading for non-Muslims, it also offers hope for disillusioned Muslims by pointing them to a knowledge of the true God."
> – Joshua Lingel, Executive Director of i2 Ministries Adjunct Professor of Islamic Studies; Biola University/Talbot School of Theology, USA

"I could not dispute the points *Who is this Allah?* made since they were firmly established in the Qur'an. I had read all the Qur'anic passages he was quoting, but until then I never realized their implications.

I began to have a new understanding… The Jesus I knew in the Qur'an was a different person than the Jesus Christ I was reading about in this book.

My heart began to open to know more about this Jesus. I then realized this might be the answer to the cry of my heart I recited everyday in my daily prayers, 'Show us the true path…' After reading the book, I chose to believe in the Jesus of the Bible and receive him as my Lord and Savior. Suddenly, I burst into tears asking God to forgive all my sins and receive me as His child."
> – Abdul Salam, Northern Nigeria

Who Is this Allah?

CHICK PUBLICATIONS
ONTARIO, CALIFORNIA

For a complete list of distributors near you,
call (909) 987-0771, or visit
www.chick.com

Copyright ©2008 G.J.O. Moshay

Published by:

CHICK PUBLICATIONS
PO Box 3500, Ontario, Calif. 91761-1019 USA
Tel: (909) 987-0771
Fax: (909) 941-8128
Web: www.chick.com
Email: postmaster@chick.com

Printed in the United States of America

ISBN: 978-07589-0715-8

CONTENTS

DEDICATION

This edition is dedicated to the thousands of innocent people from different nations who lost their lives in the terrorist attacks of September 11, 2001 in the United States of America.

It is also dedicated to the memory of all the Christians who were slaughtered in Northern Nigeria by Muslims in March 1987, and particularly to the memory of Elder Kaduzu Shebuka of the Sudan Interior Mission (SIM), who during one of the crises, was "doused with petrol and set ablaze," and burned to death in front of his church.

FOREWORD

When this book first appeared in 1990, it seemed to a number of us in Europe and the USA, that it addressed one of the most important issues of the day. Since then it has been widely circulated and has also proved a great stimulus in the debate concerning the Allah of Islam.

The debate has relevance to Christian attitudes towards Islam and to Muslim attitudes towards Christianity. It is also important to lawmakers who seek to accommodate the needs and aspirations of Muslims where, previously, Christianity was the main influence upon the laws of a country.

It is necessary, for example, that the God of Islam be understood by those who are reviewing the blasphemy laws in Britain, and by others who are responsible for teaching religious topics in schools, and still others who must make decisions regarding the building of mosques in communities.

Many people in the West have little knowledge of Islam, while many Muslims don't know the difference between the teachings of the Bible and those of the Qur'an. Hence this timely book is recommended for readership by both Muslims and non-Muslims, so the truth about Allah can be understood.

A number of Christian leaders have checked the accuracy and appropriateness of this book and thoroughly endorse it.

Dr. Clifford Denton, *MA (Cantab) D Phil (Oxon), President, Cambrian Bible College, U.K.*

PREFACE

Whether in Sunnism, Sufism, Shi'itism, Wahhabism, Ahmadiyya, or any of the one hundred and fifty sects and sub-sects of Islam, the common denominator is Allah.

Who is this Allah? Much has been written on the religion of Islam and its prophet; but not much is said about the God of the religion. One reason is the assumption that the God of Islam and the God of Christianity are one and the same.

When, on September 11, 2001, some Muslims carried out a well-organized attack, destroying the The World Trade Center and damaging the Pentagon, a letter of last instruction from the leaders of the terrorist network was discovered.

Written in Arabic, it says their mission was a service to "God." Actually this was a mistranslation. The word the terrorists used is not the Arabic word for "God" but "Allah." The Arabic word for "God" is "Ilah." So they believed they were working for "Allah," not "God."

Who is this Allah? Were these terrorists extremists, or were they serving the Allah of the Qur'an?

The war against terrorism goes beyond overthrowing the Taliban regime in Afghanistan or even killing Osama bin Laden. The war on terror may not be won unless we understand the Allah the terrorists say inspires them.

Not all Muslims are terrorists. But the terrorists' letter, which is quoted fully in chapter three, gives great insight into the Islamic religion and the motivation for religious terrorism in the world.

Why have we shied away from probing the identity of the Allah of Islam? Possibly it is because if Allah is not the God of the Bible, it would force us to face many ugly facts.

For example, if Allah is not the true God, and the Qur'an, Islam's sacred book, is true, then Christians can be sure they are lost, no matter how zealous they may be. The reverse would also be true. It is necessary, therefore, to provide sufficient information to enable you to determine your own verdict, and answer the question: Who is this Allah?

SEARCHING THE QUR'AN

The Qur'an, (sometimes spelled "Koran") is divided into 114 suras (chapters) and verses. Many English translations have been compared, especially against Abdullah Yusuf Ali's *Qur'an: Text, Translation and Commentary* (1938 ed.) and that of Drs. Muhammad T. Al-Hilali and Muhammad Muhsi Khan of the Islamic University, Medina.

One problem you may face when looking up Qur'an verses is that some chapters are not numbered the same. Some suras have more verses in one translations than in others. So if you can't find a verse in your version, check a few verses up or down. You will probably find it.

TIME TO
FACE THE FACTS

"Blessed is the nation whose God is the LORD."[1] (And blessed is the religion whose God is the LORD.)

DURING AN ELECTION CAMPAIGN, a man had a sticker on his car bumper with the inscription: *"My mind is already made up; don't confuse me with the facts."*

Many of us adopt this attitude towards some of our serious beliefs. Comforting as it may seem, this attitude can be dangerous. Some facts can be disturbing, but such disturbances and "confusions" may be necessary, especially if they concern the destiny of one's soul.

It has long been assumed that Christians and Muslims

1) Psalm 33:12.

serve the same God, and only the language of expression and mode of worship differ. This assumption can no longer continue with the popular clichés of political correctness. What we believe must be according to facts from the original sources of the religion.

When America was attacked on September 11, and about 3,000 people perished, the attackers believed they were serving Allah. Why would people die in a plane crash with so strong a conviction that they were fighting to satisfy their "God?" After fourteen centuries, and in the light of our present-day experiences, it has become necessary to study the deity of Allah and search for the real identity of the Muslim God.

The seriousness of this demands candor; but this book was not written out of bitterness or resentment against Muslims, but out of Christian love, by which we are constrained to speak the truth. The events of 9/11 give us a great opportunity to research Islam, the motivating force behind most religious terrorists in the world. It is time to re-examine our response to Islam and our responsibility towards Muslims who live in the Western world.

WHO IS ALLAH?

Is Allah God? Is he the "*God and Father of our Lord Jesus Christ*" (Colossians 1:3)? Many opinions abound. Some say yes, while some say he cannot possibly be. Others say he is a mighty god, but not the Almighty God. Some believe there are two Allahs. They say the "Allah" of the Arab, Malay, Indonesian and Hausa Christians is different than the "Allah" of the Muslims in these same areas. According to them, while the Allah of the Arab Christians is God, the Allah of the Muslims is not. But if he is not, who is he?

A lie engineered by the devil cannot be defeated by hazy and vague ideas. In a matter concerning the salvation of man's soul, there is no substitute for adequate knowledge. We must go deep into the Qur'an, *Hadith* (Islamic traditions), history and linguistics, and back to the Bible.

The most effective way to convince Muslims of the history of Islam is to quote Muslim historians, especially as contained in the *Hadith*. These traditions are many and voluminous and a study of them can be tortuous. But to be effective, we must consult these works.

But not all Muslims accept all Islamic traditions, or *Hadith,* as authentic. Therefore, we shall endeavor not to quote any tradition that contradicts the Qur'an. Those quoted shall be only to explain further what is said in the Qur'an.

The major and generally accepted *Hadiths* to both Shi'ites and Sunnis are the *Sahih Al Bukhari, Kitab al zakat* by Muslim, *Sahih Muslim, Mishkatu'l Masabih, Sirat'ur Rasul* by Ibn Ishaq, and those of Ibn Athir, Abu Daud, Abu c Abd ar-Rahmann-al-Nasa and Abu c Isa Mohammed, Jami`at Tirmidhi, Ibn Majah and Sunna An-Nasa'i.

A cosmetic treatment of the matter will only lead to a lazy conclusion which may be more confusing than convincing, and consequently, may be dangerous concerning the destiny of the souls of millions of well-meaning adherents of Islam. Efforts shall be made to discuss all brain-boiling questions that may be raised.

Until recently, Muslims were reluctant to use the English word or any other word for God. They preferred "Allah." Recently, however, many are now substituting "God" for "Allah" in modern Islamic literature. As I said in the preface, the word used in the terrorists instruction manual of 9/11 that was translated "God" is "Allah." It is different from the real Arabic word for God, which is "*Ilah*."

Such a substitution compounds the issue. If this letter had been accurately translated, some of the comments of the world leaders and Christians on the connection between Islam and the attackers may have been different.

To believe there is no difference between Allah and God is simplistic. What does the Qur'an say about this? Speaking to the Christians and Jews of his time who had some reservations on the object of worship in Islam, Muhammad said:

> …Our Alllah and your Allah is (the same) One; and it is to Him we bow (in Islam)."[2]

That is, "the Allah we prostrate and sacrifice to in Islam and the Jehovah of your Bible is the same being."

Some may accept this claim, but a serious truth-seeking Christian or Muslim who carefully studies the Qur'an and compares it with the Bible, soon discovers problems. That great scholar of Islamic religion, Samuel Zwemer, wrote:

> It is so easy to be misled by a name or by etymologies. Nearly all writers take for granted that the God of the Koran is the same being and has like attributes as Jehovah

2) Sura 29:46 (Yusuf Ali).

or as the Godhead of the New Testament.
Is this view correct?[3]

A big question indeed! Since this question was asked back in 1905, much research has been undertaken. We need to examine the facts. This may not sit well with some people, especially now, when many are discussing inter-faithism, closing their eyes to what divides the religions of the world.

In his almost prophetic classic *The Islamic Invasion*, American scholar Dr. Robert Morey says:

> The sloppy thinking that would ignore the essential differences which divide world religions is an insult to the uniqueness of world religions.[4]

A Christian professor of Islamic theology, Kenneth Cragg, in his apologetic, *The Call of the Minaret*, says:

> Those who say that Allah is not "the God and Father of our Lord Jesus Christ" are right if they mean God is not so described by Muslims. They are wrong if they mean that Allah is other than the God of the Christian faith.[5]

On the surface, this observation seems to settle the matter. But the issue is not so simple to be dismissed in those two sentences. The problem lies in the origin of the Qur'an. Are the claims in the Qur'an mere apprehensions of the Divine

3) Zwemer, Samuel, *The Muslim Doctrine of God: An Essay on the Character of Allah According to the Koran*, New York: American Tract Society, 1905.
4) Morey, Robert. *The Islamic Invasion*, Oregon: Harvest House, 1992, p. 53.
5) Cragg, K. *The Call of the Minaret* Ibadan: Daystar Press, 1985, p. 30.

from Muhammad's head? Was the message in the Qur'an received or conceived?

We must understand that although there could be a philosophy of religion, religion is basically not a philosophy but a revelation. It cannot be judged on the same pedestal as the Platonic, Socratic, Cartesian or other philosophies. Islam, in particular, is a religion of revelation (ARABIC: *wahy* or *naql*), at least at its inception. It would be helpful to realize that the difference between Allah and the God of the Christian faith is not just of description as Professor Cragg suggests.

Muslims do not say they are describing Allah. In fact, Allah cannot be described. A Muslim can only raise his hands to the sky or bow down in adoration and say, "*Allahu Akbar!* (literally, 'Allah is the Greater')." He is too great to be described by human beings.

Even his "99 Most Beautiful Names" in the Qur'an are not descriptions by human beings. They are revelations by Allah himself. Muhammad did not just conceive the Allah in the Qur'an. Conception is a person's own idea about a thing (Arabic: *aql*); it is a product of man.

According to Muslims, and the Qur'an, Islam did not originate from Muhammad's consciousness. He might have gotten a conception of God before, but the religion of Islam is a direct revelation, and not a product of a philosophical genius. Muhammad was only a prophet. According to Islam, everything in the Qur'an is a Divine Revelation (*tanzil*) that is, something "sent down" (Sura 53:4).

Muhammad did not write the Qur'an. After all, he was an *Ummi* (unlettered, stark illiterate, Sura 7:158). His childhood was marked with abject poverty, so he possibly did not go to school. How then could he have written such a wonderful book?

The Qur'an supposedly descended from heaven, and the original copy is still on the "Preserved Tablet" (*Lauh Mahfuz*) or "Mother of the Book" (*Umul al Kitab*) in Paradise, and was there even before the creation of the world. Because of this, nothing in the book must be questioned.[6]

The Western mind may find all this unbelievable. But take them away, and there would be nothing called Islam. This is what several million Muslims believe, and we will base our study on these beliefs.

The Allah in the Qur'an is therefore a revealed Allah and not just a conception (*aql*) emanating from Muslim's heads. Contrary to what Cragg says, it is not the Christians who say Allah is not "the God and Father of our Lord Jesus Christ." Whoever Allah is or is not, is a revelation of the Qur'an rather than the claims of Christians.

The God of the Bible is not a description either. He revealed Himself to Abram, Jacob, Moses, the Prophets, and came down to manifest Himself physically in the Person of Jesus of Nazareth. Jesus said: *"He that hath seen me hath seen the Father."* (John 14:9).

Christians and the Jews did not conceive of the God of the Bible. God revealed Himself: His nature, His Name, His

6) Suras 85:22 and 43:3-4.

glory, His law, His judgment, His love, His holiness. Take away these revelations, and there would be nothing called Judaism or Christianity.

Today, Christians know God as He is in the Bible and in their lives. Likewise, Allah is known (supposedly) to Muslims as he is in the Qur'an, and as he manifests himself in their lives. These revelations and manifestations (not descriptions) determine the Islamic ethos and the Christian ethics.

Therefore, the problem before us is not that of conflicting descriptions of the Divine, but of revelations. And since these revelations are contained in the two books, the Qur'an and the Bible, they shall form the basic texts of identifying who Allah is. There is no other way.

We intend to explain the Qur'an as it is, with all its claims, comparing Allah, the major character, with the Christian God. We need to have our minds open, not afraid of being disturbed with the facts. Such disturbances are necessary. Sometimes we need to be upset before we can be set up.

We should note that many Muslims resent a non-Muslim quoting from their sacred book for fear of an un-Islamic interpretation. But if the Qur'an contains clear facts and is the Word of God for the salvation of mankind, people must be free to read it and refer to it in a religious discourse.

In the Bible, God allows even Satan(!) to quote from His Word (Matthew. 4:5-7). But in quoting from the Qur'an, we will not agree with Al-A`shari that the Qur'an should be accepted *bi-la kayf* i.e. "without asking questions." In Sura 5:101 of the Qur'an, Allah gives Muslims a strict warning:

O you who believe! (Muslims), Ask not
(questions) about things which, if made
plain to you, may cause you trouble....

The devil's greatest weapon is ignorance. That is why
the first weapon of spiritual warfare listed in Ephesians 6
is the "belt of truth," so to speak. If we are to get free from
the enemy of our lives, we must get the truth.

This will involve probing things we have long assumed,
and questioning a book that claims divine origin. If we desire
the truth, we must reject the Islamic concept of "Ta abbudi,"
that the Qur'an must "be accepted without criticism."[7]

In the Qur'anic verse quoted above, Allah warns that if
some things in the Qur'an are made clear, they may cause
trouble for the Muslim. But the Islamic world cannot continue to live in ignorance through the "blasphemy" threats
of their leaders. Many young Muslim thinkers today want
the "troubles" of plain truths to begin! They have to ask
questions. And the first question we need to ask is:

WHO WROTE THE QUR'AN?

The Qur'an's authorship has been treated in detail in a
separate book by this author.[8] But the issue needs a push here.
Most Muslims believe the Qur'an came down from heaven
and was given to Muhammad as a book or sheets in stages.
The Qur'an claims in many verses that it came down from
Allah through the angel Gabriel (cf. Sura 3:3; 4:105)[9.]

7) Gibb, H. A. R & Kramers, *Dictionary of Islam*, p. 525.
8) Moshay, G.J.O. *Anatomy of the Qur'an* (2007). Chick Publications.
9) Muhammad Haykal, *The Life of Muhammad*, Islamic Publications Bureau,
Lagos, p. 73.

If we try to determine the Qur'an's authorship from its claims, however, we may not succeed. For example, Suras 26:192-194 and 16:102 say Muhammad received the Qur'an from "the Holy Spirit." But Suras 53:2-18 and 81:19-24 say "one Mighty in Power"[10] personally delivered the already written book to Muhammad, and Muhammad saw him.

Elsewhere we read that Angel Gabriel brought the Qur'an down from heaven and handed it to Muhammad or brought it to his heart (cf. Sura 2:97). In Sura 15:8, we are told that it was "angels," not Allah, Gabriel or the "Holy Spirit."

If a Muslim reader is confused, he has reasons to be. So let us agree on one point. Some enlightened Muslims believe it would be more reasonable to regard the book as the written form of the verbal message given to Muhammad, and so a revelation.

Reading the comments of most Islamic scholars who translated the Qur'an, one easily sees that, apart from their stereotypical romanticism, they, too, are not sure of the authorship of the book.

A careful student who reads it in Arabic or in translations will see that, apart from direct quotes from reported events, some parts of the narratives are in the first person plural, some are in the third person and some in the first person singular. There are places where Allah is being addressed by the writer. The writer seems to forget he should maintain the narrative as coming from Allah and suddenly changes it.

---

10) Some commentators, like Yusuf Ali, aware of the contradiction, suggest that "the One Mighty in power" is Gabriel. But how can Muhammad give such a title to Gabriel? Only God can be so described.

For example, when the speaker-writer says: "I swear by Allah that they will not believe…" one wonders who is speaking, Allah or a writer? How can Allah "swear by Allah"? Or how could these statements have existed in heaven in a book before Creation?

Some historians have attempted to prove that the Qur'an was not written by Muhammad, or even during his lifetime. They say he was illiterate and the Qur'an is a product of some zealots of Islam under the supervision of a caliph.

After their master's death, they felt they must have a sacred book just as Christians and Jews have. So they recalled what their leader had preached before his death. Part of it is said to be from the parchment he wrote and before his death.

According to the *Hadith*, some of the fragments were collected from "tablets of stone, ribs of palm branches, camels' shoulder-blades and ribs, pieces of board, and the breasts of men, (that is from men's memory)."

The first attempt of compilation is said to have been made by Muhammad's daughter, Fatima, who had to contest some of the facts with some followers of her father since different people were reciting different versions.

Muhammad's wife, Hafsa, also helped in the compilation. The final work, however, is credited to Zaid ibn Thabit, whom some believe was merely the editor.

Because of the predominant use of the first person plural and singular narratives, we will accept for now that there was a being from whom Muhammad was receiving his messages, and this being is called "Allah" in Arabic; and that even if the book was written by the followers after his death, it is not impossible to remember some of the words of Muhammad when he was being inspired to recite the Qur'an.

This position is necessary to establish our logic. If we accept the Qur'an as divinely inspired by some being, we should not be afraid to identify that being. If we say no supernatural being spoke to Muhammad or at least inspired him to say what he said, we would have no choice but to dismiss the whole Qur'an and regard Muhammad as one of the most successful liars and deceivers the world has ever seen.

But that is not the case because, throughout the Qur'an, Allah is quoted exhaustively as the one speaking, even in the first person plural, signifying a dignified or honorific personality or deity.

So we take a stand: there was an Allah talking to or inspiring Muhammad. The issue is whether this Allah is the Jehovah of the Bible.

We cannot impose an opinion. There are sufficient facts in this book for you to determine your own conclusion. But it is important for the Muslim reader to be very honest with himself and read the book through because this is a serious matter that has an eternal consequence for his soul.

If a Muslim finds the answer to the question, "who is this Allah of Islam?" his life will change forever!

ALLAH AND VIOLENCE

CHAPTER TWO

WE MUST bear in mind that Islam is spiritual, so a mere academic discussion will lead us nowhere. It is easy for those who only hear about the violence and mysticism in Islam to explain away the religion on exegetical levels. The other easy way out is to find a political explanation.

But violence in Islam is real and is spiritual. This is very serious, yet it is a fact. No matter how trenchant this may be, many honest Muslims are ready to examine the facts and apply reason and not just get flared up emotionally.

Many Muslims are embarrassed about the violence done in the name of their religion and explain that Islam is being misrepresented by these violent people. We honestly wish this were so.

We often hear that Islam is a religion of peace; that only

the extremists are violent. But we rarely ask ourselves whether what we say about a religion is according to history or our expectation of the religion, or according to the modern slogans of Islamic leaders and our politicians.

ISLAM'S HISTORY

The history of Islam, written by the most respected and earliest Muslim historians does not show the kind of Islam Americans expect. The sacred books of Islam, the Qur'an and the body of tradition called the *Hadith*, show clearly the real Islam. Any other "Islam" is our own imaginations and expectations.

In this chapter, we will show that the actions of Islamic terrorists are not necessarily because they are evil. Rather, it is because of who they believe to be "God" speaking in the Qur'an. They follow his clear instruction and motivation.

Islam is what the founder of the religion says it is, and not what politicians and American academics think it is. The best example of Islam is not seen in any modern man, but in its founder.

Many of Muslims are nice people who normally would not practice violence. But the more a Muslim studies and understands the Qur'an, and the history of Islam's founder, the more he realizes that non-Muslims must be forced to accept Islam or be subjugated if they ignore the religion.

In this chapter, we will see the teaching of the Qur'an on "the peace" of Islam; and the founder's position on terrorism.

MUSLIMS AND CHRISTIANS: ENEMIES?

Matters on religion are complex. In a speech on the need for the peaceful co-existence of Muslims and Christians, particularly in Nigeria, former military ruler General Ibrahim Babangida of Nigeria wrote:

> It may be a theological question whether God reveals himself or he reveals religion through his messenger, his prophet or his son. Irrespective of the position one takes on this issue, one should be reasonable enough to know that God, like the father of any household, can never be satisfied with members of the family who quarrel, fight, undermine and sometimes kill one another in his name.[1]

Many people know what they think God is supposed to be, yet may be serving a wrong "God" with all sincerity. Many find themselves in a system that is difficult to leave. Others do not see the need to leave their religious system because they are ignorant of the deception they have fallen into. But if they will patiently journey through the pages of this book, they may have to rethink what they believe.

General Babangida's pronouncement was made from an honest mind: "…God can never be satisfied with quarreling, fighting, undermining, killing in his name." That is true. But which God? The Bible's God, or Allah? Or are they the same? That is the real "theological question."

1) *New Nigerian,* Kaduna: October 19, 1988, p. 3.

The other "theological question" the General raised is the definition of "the family" and "the household." Babangida is a Muslim, and he needs to remember that according to Islamic thought, there are two distinct households in the world: the *Dar ul-Islam* ('household of Islam'), and *Dar ul-Harb* ('household of non-Islam or war').

Because they are two distinct households, they surely don't have the same father. And because Christians are non-Muslims, they naturally belong to the latter household, the *Dar ul-Harb*.

So when Babangida says "the family," "the household," is he referring to the different sects in Islam, or to Christians and Muslims? Can he prove that Muslims are in the same family or household with Christians? Do the Qur'an or *Hadith* say so?

When a Muslim kills a Christian, is he killing "one another" or is he getting rid of a *kaferi* (infidel)? All these questions must be answered *from the Qur'an* and the *Hadith* and not from personal religious opinions.

When a Muslim says, "Islam has a full-fledged philosophy of religious tolerance and peaceful coexistence,"[2] he is either deceiving or is not well informed about the history and teaching of his religion. When Christians or Western leaders say this, it is because they have been deceived.

Whatever we say about Islam must be established from the Qur'an and the *Hadith*. Some of us have studied the

2) Babangida, I. B. "Man has Failed Islam and Christianity," *The Guardian*, Lagos, August 14, 1992, p. 31.

Qur'an from cover to cover again and again. We have also read many of the *Hadiths*. We have not seen this philosophy of tolerance and peace in these books.

The only verse a Muslim can confidently point to as "tolerant verse" in the Qur'an is Sura 2:256 which says in part, *"Let there be no compulsion in religion."* But this statement was made at the early stage of Muhammad's mission, when he was just settling down in Yathrib (Medina). Such an attitude was necessary to get the cooperation of the Jews and Christians who were in the majority in Yathrib.

Muhammad said he believed in all the Jewish prophets, and that he had not brought any new religion but the same things the old prophets of Israel had preached. At that time, he did not have enough people to wage a war. However, when he raised enough military manpower, he launched out against those he suspected did not believe in his religion.

Muslims are commanded by Allah (or whoever is speaking in the Qur'an) to smite the neck of anyone who does not accept the teachings of Islam. According to the verses, they would be helping Allah by so doing:

> So when you meet (in fight *Jihad* in Allah's
> Cause), those who disbelieve smite at (their)
> necks till when you have killed and wounded
> many of them, then bind a bond firmly (on
> them, i.e. take them as captives). Thereafter
> (is the time) either for generosity (i.e. free
> them without ransom), or ransom (accord-
> ing to what benefits Islam), until the war
> lays down its burden. Thus [you are ordered

> by Allah to continue in carrying out *Jihad*
> against the disbelievers <u>*till they embrace*</u>
> <u>*Islam*</u> (i.e. are saved from the punishment
> in the Hell-fire) or at least come under your
> protection], but if it had been Allah's Will,
> He Himself could certainly have punished
> them (without you)...[3]

In Sura 9:19 Allah explains that Jihad (with belief in Allah and the Last Day) attracts more rewards than other religious duties in Islam.

It is important to stress that much of our discussion is *not* from Western historians but from the Qur'an and Islamic traditions called the *Hadith* and from the present experiences in many parts of the world. Please check these references because most Muslims accuse non-Muslim writers of quoting the Qur'an out of context if they do not like the point being proven.

Even though many killings were done by Muslims when the religion came to Medina, not all Muslims were initially interested in fighting Jews, Christians or their fellow Mecca kinsmen, or looting their caravans to spread a religion.

In Sura 4:74-80, many Arab Muslims protested Muhammad's call for Jihad (Muslim holy war), saying, "Our Lord! Why has thou ordered us to fight? (v. 77)" But Muhammad convinced them his command was directly from Allah.

Allah says Jihad is not just a religious duty but a profitable business (Sura 61:10-12). The *Hadith* says Jihad is:

3) Sura 47:4 (Hilali and Khan).

...the best method of earning (blessings)
both spiritual and temporal. If victory is
won, there is enormous booty of a country,
which cannot be equaled to any other source
of income. If there is defeat or death, there
is everlasting paradise...[4]

It is therefore clear that physical Jihad is NOT extremism or fanaticism but normal in Muhammad's original Islam.

JIHAD ON CONVERTS FROM ISLAM

Article 18 of the International Covenant on Civil and Political Rights 1966 says everyone:

"shall have the right to freedom of thought,
conscience and religion. This right shall
include *freedom to have or to adopt a
religion* or belief of his choice, and freedom,
either individually or in community with
others and in public or private, to manifest
his religion or belief in worship, observance,
practice and teaching."

Article 18 of the Universal Declaration of Human Rights 1948 says the same thing about freedom of religion:

"...this right includes freedom to change
his religion or belief..."

Islamic nations signed this Covenant, but many of them do not follow it. Some have a kind of "freedom of religion"

---

4) *Mishkat Masabih* Vol. II, p. 253, cited in Gerhard Nehls, *A Guide to Muslim Evangelism*, Life Challenge, Nairobi, p. 4.

in their constitutions, but it is not granted in practice. Their "freedom of religion" means freedom to join and remain a Muslim, but not freedom to leave Islam!

It is a criminal offence in countries like Saudi Arabia, Iran, Sudan, Mauritania, Qatar, Yemen and a few others for a Muslim to change his religion. To leave Islam is regarded as high treason and punishable by death.

Saudi Arabian citizen, Sidiq Mulallah, was beheaded by the Saudi government in September 1992 for changing his faith from Islam to Christianity.

Ghorban Tori, a convert from Islam to Christianity in Iran was arrested on 22 November 2005 by government security forces for this change of faith. A few hours later, he was found stabbed to death in front of his home.

In December 1990, Rev. Hussein Soodmand was hanged in an official execution by the Iranian authorities. He was buried in a cemetery for outcasts "where dogs go." His offense: he left Islam for Christianity. Several such killings are going on, many of them secretly organized.

Are these Islamic governments extremists or they are practicing the Islam of Allah in the Qur'an? Let Allah speak:

> They wish that you should reject Faith (Islam), as they have rejected (Faith), and thus that you all become equal (like one another). So take not friends from them, till they emigrate in the Way of Allah (to Muhammad). But if they turn back (from Islam), take (hold) of them and kill them

> wherever you find them, and take neither
> friends or helpers from them.[5]

According to this Islamic injunction, any Muslim who turns apostate, i.e. abandons Islam for another religion, must be killed; he is seen as a traitor, an enemy of Islam and the Prophet of Islam. Any Muslims, especially his immediate family members, have the power to plant their sword in him.

First, this sentence was used for non-Muslims who were converted to Islam and later turned away it. Later it became a weapon against those born and raised in the religion.

An American Muslim who is not aware of this aspect of Islam may say, "You are misinterpreting the word of Allah and his messenger." Let us hear the interpretation of the Prophet of Allah himself. In the *Hadith* of Al-Bukhari we read:

> "The Prophet said: 'If somebody (a Muslim)
> discards his religion, kill him.'"[6]

Now, do we need a Chief Imam to tell us the "real" meaning of this instruction?

This same *Hadith* of Al-Bukhari gives records of the execution of people who left Islam for another religion.[7] Here there are also strict warnings of death to those who might be contemplating leaving Islam.

In Volume 4, #814 of this *Hadith*, Muhammad says that when a Muslim abandons Islam, becomes a Christian, then

5) Sura 4:89 (Hilali and Khan).
6) The *Hadith* of Al-Bukhari, *The Translation of the Meaning of Sahih Al-Bukhari*, translated by Dr. Muhammad Muhsin Khan, Professor of Arabic language at the Islamic University of Medina, Vol. 5, #261.
7) See Vol. 5, #630; also Vol. 9, #10-11, 26, 45-50, 341-342.

dies and is buried, the earth will reject his corpse and keep throwing it out of the grave.

Even though Sura 16:106 says the apostate from Islam should be given over to the wrath of Allah, faithful Muslims are mandated by Allah to execute his wrath on wrongdoers.

An American Christian missionary once asked a Muslim what he would you do if his son became a Christian. "I'd cut his throat," said the man.[8]

We know such is not the case in many families. But it is always very costly for anyone from a serious Islamic family to be converted, especially to the Christian faith. The more a man is familiar with what Allah says in the Qur'an and what Muhammad says in the *Hadith*, the more he sees his responsibility to deal with someone who leaves Islam.

From my own experience working among Muslims in many parts of the world, I can say that the greatest hindrance to a Muslim's decision to follow Christ is FEAR of what other Muslims would do to them. Even when Muslims are convicted of their sins, or convinced of the truth of the Christian faith, they still fear the implications of conversion.

Most former Muslims who are Christians today have stories to tell in this regard[9.] Many of them are disowned. We know of a case of parents poisoning their daughter for denouncing Islam and becoming a Christian. A letter from someone who uses our books for evangelism among Muslims in an Islamic stronghold says:

---

8) Sumrall, Lester, *Where Was God When Pagan Religions Began?*, Nashville: Thomas Nelson, 1980, p. 138.
9) Moshay, (ed). *How We Found Jesus: 20 Ex-Muslims Testify.*

> …A man here got converted… and since
> he still lived in the family house, his par-
> ents (as usual here) parked all his personal
> belongings and put fire on them while he
> was away at his job.

What about a father who stripped his three daughters naked because they became Christian? He cast them out of the house and asked people to stone them. To worsen the sight, one of them was in her menstrual period. After, they were locked up in a room for three days without food or water. Then their father had their brother serve them poisoned rice. Because they did not die, their brother also gave his life to Christ.

Today, the three ladies are all married to pastors. The father, too, "soft-pedaled" later but was reluctant to confess the Christian faith openly because of what other Muslims would do to him.

These may be uncommon cases, but we must never imagine that such Muslim fathers were being unnecessarily wicked. They were simply being faithful to their religion.

Much of the incitement to violence and war in the Qur'an is directed against Jews and Christians who rejected the strange god Muhammad was preaching.

It wasn't long before pagan Arabians submitted to Islam since Allah was one of several gods of the people. But Jews and Christians were recalcitrant, feeling they had a better God. They were reluctant to accept what they perceived as one of the pantheons of Arabia. They probably remembered the Scripture that *"For ALL the gods of the people* (in whatever guise) *are idols… "* [10]

In plain terms, Muhammad or Allah (or whoever is speaking in the Qur'an) says:

> O you who believe! Take not the Jews and
> the Christians as friends, they are but friends
> to one another. And if any amongst you
> takes them as (friends), then surely he is
> one of them. Verily, Allah guides not those
> people who are unjust. [11]

In other words, any Muslim who becomes a Christian or even befriends a Christian, leaves the leadership and control of Allah. This is not Ghaddafi, Khomeini or Osma bin Laden talking. This is Allah talking through Muhammad.

So all Islamic leaders who come to some British or American church leaders for inter-faith co-operation are either defying the instructions of Allah or they have a hidden agenda. The Islam of the 7th century A.D. is the same today, probably under new guises as the situation demands.

It is the same tactic of "There is no compulsion in religion" that Muhammad first adopted to Christians and Jews that Muslims are using in the Western world today. First, they settle down as strangers. But when they are established, we may begin to see another side. This is their basic strategy:

• Migrate to Christian areas because they are tolerant. Pretend to be peaceful, friendly and hospitable.

10) 1 Chronicles 16:26.
11) Sura 5:51 (Hilali and Khan). v, 54 in Yusuf Ali; Suras 2:120; 9:5, 29, 123.

• When you settle in, clamor for religious, political and social rights and privileges that Christians are not allowed in an Islamic country.

• Breed fast and acquire much property. As you increase in a particular area, insist that there should be no Christian activities in your community. You may speak or write to discredit their religion, but they must not talk about Islam.

• Expand your community; Christian activities should be restricted in all the places you expand to.

• The moment you have enough military might against these "disbelievers," these trinitarian *kaferis*, eliminate them or suppress them as much as you can, and be in control.

Where immediate invasion is not possible, that has always been the policy. There are so many incitements against Christians and non-Muslims running through the pages of the Qur'an we find it hard to believe that any practicing Muslim or follower of the Qur'an and the *Hadith* could not hate Christians in some way. It means he has not gotten the spirit of Islam.

If a Muslim expects to get rewards in the Muslim heaven how else should he behave but obey Allah in the Qur'an?

> "Let those fight in the way of Allah who sell
> the life of this world for the other. *Whoso*
> *fighteth in the way of Allah, be he slain or*
> *be he victorious, on him We shall bestow a*
> *vast reward...*
>
> Hast thou not seen those unto whom it was
> said: Withold your hands, establish worship

> and pay the poordue (charity), but when
> fighting was prescribed for them behold! a
> party of them fear mankind even as their
> fear of Allah or with greater fear…"[12]

This indicates that submission to Allah is not just in prayers and *zakat* as some want us to believe, but in obedience to the order to kill in order to spread. Was this not the original Islam?

In the *Hadith* Mishkat,[13] the mother of Haritha was assured by Muhammad that Haritha had attained the highest garden in Paradise because he died while fighting for Islam. In the same *Hadith*, Muhammad also said:

> He who dies without having fought, or
> having felt it to be his duty will die guilty
> of a kind of hypocrisy.

> The last hour will not come before the
> Muslims fight the Jews and the Muslims
> kill them.

How then can the Allah of Muhammad be the same God of the Jews? Muhammad continued:

> Three people are all in Allah's safekeeping:
> a man who goes out to fight in Allah's path,
> who is in Allah's safekeeping till Allah takes
> his soul and brings him to paradise, or sends
> him home with the reward or booty he has
> obtained…

---

12) Sura 4:74, 77 (Pickthall).
13) *Mishkat at Masabih*, Sh. M. Ashraf, (1990) pp. 147, 721, 810, 811, 1130.

Abu Dharr said he asked Muhammad what action was most excellent. He replied, "Faith in Allah and jihad (fighting) in His path." The *Hadith* of Kanz Al-Muttaqi contains the following excerpts:

> A day and a night of fighting on the frontier is better than a month of fasting and prayer.
>
> Swords are the keys of Paradise.
>
> Paradise is under the shadow of swords.
>
> He who draws his sword in the path of Allah has sworn allegiance to Allah.
>
> The unbeliever and the one who kills him will never meet in Hell.
>
> Allah sent me as a mercy and a portent; He did not send me as a trader or as a cultivator. The worst community on the Day of Resurrection are the traders and the cultivators except those (of them) who are niggardly with their religion.
>
> Go in the name of Allah and in Allah and in the religion of the Prophet of Allah! Do not kill the very old, the infant, the child or the woman. Bring all the booty, holding back no part of it. Maintain order and do good, for Allah loves those who do good.

If you find a tithe collector, kill him.[14]

Expel the Jews and the Christians from the Arabian Peninsula....[15]

Liberal Muslim scholars who are getting embarrassed by the amount of terrorism being perpetrated in the world today by Muslims try to explain Jihad away, saying physical fighting was never part of the "original" Islam, and that this was a misinterpretation of Allah's injunction by some fanatical Muslims of this generation.

This is the same opinion of many American and European opinion leaders. The facts prove that this "original Islam" is something other than what Muhammad practiced and what is inside the Qur'an and the various *Hadiths*. Our beliefs about Islam should be based on what is in the Qur'an, the *Hadith* and the historical antecedents, and not what we think Islam should be.

Many Westerners are bothered about the Islamic terrorism in the world today because they are so engrossed in tolerance that they are ignorant of history. We have been paying dearly for this ignorance. Dr. Jane Smith of Harvard University clearly showed that even the term "Islam" did not originally mean "submission"[16.]

In *The Spiritual Background of Islam,* Middle East scholar

14) We believe "tithe collector" means a clergyman, probably the Christian bishops in Nejran, Southern Arabia. Muhammad began to collect more than tithes later.
15) *Hadith* of Kanz Al-Muttaqi, Vol. II, pp. 252-286.
16) Smith, Jane, *An Historical and Semitic Study of the Term "Islam" as Seen in a Sequence of Qur'an Commentaries,* University of Montana Press, for Harvard University. Dissertations, 1970.

Dr. M. Bravmann reveals that the term "Islam" did not originally mean Muhammad's religion or that of any Jewish patriarchal religion as claimed by Muslims. According to Dr. Bravmann, the word "Islam" was *a secular concept denoting a sublime virtue in the eyes of the primitive Arab; defiance of death, heroism; to die in battle.* The term denoted bravery in battle, not "peace" or "submission."

Marshal Hodgson reminds us that the English word "assassin" is purely of Arabic origin. It was originally "Hash-shashin," (or *assassinus* in Latin) meaning "smokers of hash-ish." It referred to a certain sect of Muslims in the 11th-13th centuries who took hashish (hemp) to receive enough energy to fight for Allah by killing non-Muslims.[17]

Islam is what it was in history and what it is today; it is not our personal opinions. What many of us today call normal Islam is our own creation and not the Islam of Muhammad.

HOW JIHAD BEGAN

Muhammad's wealthy wife, Khadija bint Khuwaylid, and his powerful uncle, Abu Talib, both of whom the Meccans feared, died in the same year, within thirty days of each other. This was a big blow to Muhammad. Naturally, he felt insecure, which was why he had to flee to Taif and later to Yathrib (Medina). Those who fled with him soon settled down. The people of Yathrib welcomed them and were generous to them. But this could not continue forever.

17) Hodgson, M., *The Order of Assassins*, Gravenhage: Mouton & Co., 1955.

Life soon became difficult for these immigrants economically. Muhammad therefore felt he had to take revenge on the Meccan merchants for the hostility he had suffered in Mecca. But because of their ethnic affiliation, many of the Muslims did not see why they should attack and loot their own tribesmen in order to survive or because of a religion.

A revelation came to Muhammad from Allah to justify this first mobilization for Jihad. In the Qur'an we read:

> Jihad (holy fighting in Allah's Cause) is ordained for you (Muslims) though you dislike it, and it may be that you dislike a thing which is good for you and that you like a thing which is bad for you. Allah knows but you do not know.[18]

With this revelation, Muslims set out for their first Jihad and defeated and looted these Meccans. (This was the Nakhla Raid before the popular Battle of Badr.) The booty carried from these Meccans encouraged further Jihads. The Meccans, in retaliation, mobilized about 1,000 fighters against Muhammad. With only about 300 people, the Muslims tactically defeated the Meccans. This was the Battle of Badr.

These victories seemed to them a proof that Allah was supporting them, and that he truly sent Muhammad.

Later, Muhammad and the Meccans made covenants not to fight for a period, especially during sacred months. All these covenants were cancelled later by Muhammad, together with those made with the Jews in Yathrib.

18) Sura 2:216 (Hilali and Khan).

Let us hear the words of Shaykh (Sheikh) Abdullah bin Muhammad bin Hamid the Chief Justice of Saudi Arabia:

> Then Allah revealed in Sura Bara'at (Repentance, IX) the order to discard (all) obligations (covenants), etc, and commanded the Muslims to fight all the pagans as well as against the people of the Scriptures (Jews and Christians) <u>if they do not embrace Islam</u>,[19] till they pay the Jizya (A tax levied on those who do not embrace Islam).

> Muslims were not permitted to abandon "the fighting" against them (pagans, Jews and Christians) and to reconcile with them and to suspend hostilities against them for an unlimited period while they are strong and have the possibility of fighting against them.

Shaykh bin Hamid continues:

> So at first, "the fighting" was FORBIDDEN, then it was PERMITTED, and after that it was made OBLIGATORY. Allah gave importance to the subject matter of Jihad in ALL the suras (Chapters of the Qur'an) which made "the fighting" (Jihad) obligatory for Muslims and gave the suras revealed (at Medina) as it is in Allah's state-

19) Christians and Jews were to be killed *"...if they do not embrace Islam."* This contradicts the claims of some modern Muslim revisionists. Jihad against Christians was NOT defensive but offensive. Read Sura 9:29, 123.

ment: "March forth whether you are light
(being healthy, young and wealthy) or heavy
(being ill, old and poor) and strive hard with
your wealth and your lives in the cause of
Allah. That is better for you if you (but)
knew" (Sura 9:41 emphasis mine).[20]

Many Muslims never like reading about the violence and
terrorism in Islam as though this were a misrepresentation.
But can they ignore their history?

Muhammad not only commanded wars, but was also
involved personally. During his lifetime, 66 battles were
fought by his troop, of which he personally led 27. It was
on a battleground (Battle of Uhud, 625 A.D.) that Muhammad broke one of his teeth. Some traditions say two front
teeth.

Islam is the exposition of its prophet. The real Islam is
the life of Muhammad. If we ignore the history of Muhammad, then we are creating our own personal religion and not
the Islam of history.

Some Muslim apologists tell us that the wars Muhammad fought were political rather than religious. From the
quotations above, we know this claim has no foundation. In
any case, Islam draws no distinction between religion and
politics… a fact America has not fully grasped.

If Muhammad was alive today and practicing and spreading his Islam, whatever impression we had of Ayatollah Kho-

20) Sahykh Abdullah bn Muhammad bn Hamid, *The Call to Jihad: Striving
for Allah's Cause.* This publication is also attached to the Hilali and Khan
Qur'an translation.

meini is what many Americans would have of him. Many of our Christian and political leaders would regard him as not practicing the "real Islam."

ISLAM AND LITERARY EXPOSURE

Independent-thinking writers are dangerous to Islam. A number of writers who criticize Islam today have lost their freedom; some even losing their lives in Islamic countries. Egyptian writer, Farag Fouda, was murdered early in 1992 by Muslims for criticizing Islamic militancy and terrorism. The Speaker of the country's Parliament was assassinated in 1990 for his anti-Islamic stance, and the militant Muslims claimed responsibility.[21]

Muslims never like anybody revealing the real history of their religion. But this is not strange. Among the first blood shed by Muhammad's followers in Yathrib was that of a poetess, Asma, daughter of Merwan and wife of Yazid bin Zaid.

According to Ibn Ishaq in his monumental work *Sirat'l Rasul*, translated and edited by Ibn Hisham as *The Life of the Prophet*, Mrs. Asma Yazid had composed and popularized some poems to ridicule the people of Yathrib for following a man who had slain 49 of his own tribesmen at Nakhla and looted their caravan in order to establish a religion.

This woman poet was stabbed on her bed by "Umayr ibn "Awf. In the words of Muslim scholar Muhammad Haykal:

---

21) *International Business Week* magazine, Berkshire: Nov. 1992, p. 20.

> Umayr ibn Awf attacked her during the
> night while she was surrounded by her
> children, one of whom she was nursing.
> "Umayr was weak of sight and had to grope
> for her. After removing the child from his
> victim, he killed her; he then proceeded
> to the Prophet and informed him of what
> he had done.[22]

He received a commendation for having done a good job for Allah. The necks of about three other poets who could not be silent faced the sharp edge of the Islamic sword and lost their heads. One of them was Abu Afk.

Another poet (and soldier), Abbas, faced a similar judgment after the Battle of Honain. The problem arose as to how Muhammad shared the booty. Abbas, said to be a "lukewarm convert," grumbled about the Apostle's arithmetic in sharing the booty, and registered his complaint in a few verses:

> The Apostle overheard him and said with
> a smile, "Take that man from here and cut
> out his tongue.[23]

AYATOLLAH KHOMEINI

Even though Ayatollah Khomeini belonged to the Shiite sect of Islam, he was generally regarded as an exemplary Muslim. Following the footsteps of the prophet of Allah in establishing an Islamic state, Khomeini slaughtered more

22) Haykal, Muhammad. *The Life of Muhammad.* North American Trust Publications, 1976, p. 243.
23) M. Ebrahim Khan, *Anecdotes From Islam,* Sh. Muhammad Ashraf, Lahore (1960), p. 20; 2. Ibn Ishaq in Sirat'ul Rasul, Vol. 3, pp. 90-91.

people during the first few years of his reign than during all the years of his predecessor, Shah Muhammad Reza Pahlavi.

After all the massacres of non-Muslims in Persia (present Iran), Khomeini said:

> "In Persia no people have been killed so far —only beasts!"[24]

On another occasion, this servant of Allah said:

> "The purest joy in Islam is to kill and be killed for Allah."[25]

Early in 1984, Ayatollah Khomeini said:

> In order to achieve the victory of Islam in the world, we need to provoke repeated crises, restore value to the idea of death and martyrdom. If Iran has to vanish, that is not important. The important thing is to engulf the world in crises....[26]

From our study of the Qur'an so far, did Khomeini sound un-Qur'anic or un-Allahic? Was he being fanatical? Is it possible that many political and Christian leaders in America and Europe know Islam better than Muhammad? Do they know Islam more than Khomeini?

If Muhammad was here today, our political leaders, the press and even some of our church leaders would tell us he was not practicing the real Islam.

24 *Who Is This Allah in Islam?* Cha. 2, Islam - A theocentric culture. See also www.wrmea.com/backissues/0489/8904003.html
25) Lamb, David: *The Arabs*, Random House, New York, (1987) p. 287.
26) *Le Point* Magazine, No. 599, March 12, 1984, pp. 89, 91.

Serious Muslims are morbidly worried about the way Christianity is growing today. South African Indian Muslim jihadist, Ahmed Deedat (now dead), was worried that:

> "Kuwait (a Muslim country) had just one Arab Christian family about fifty years ago. Today there are thirty-five churches (when he wrote this) in that little country...."[27]

He was obsessed that, in the Muslim country of Indonesia, there are 6,000 full-time foreign Christian missionaries "harassing" non-Christians. He decried the way Christianity is growing especially in Africa and therefore reminded Muslims to go back to the original Islam given by Allah in the Qur'an:

> "Our armor, sword and shield in this battle of Faiths are in the Koran, we have been chanting it (sic.) for centuries... now we must bring them forth into the battlefield...."[28]

What are these "armor, sword and shield in this battle of faiths?" Of course, they are physical armor, physical swords and all available modern weapons of warfare.

Shaykh Abdullah bin Muhammad bin Hamid of the Central Mosque of Mecca and Chief Justice of Saudi Arabia, wrote:

> To get ready (for Jihad) includes various kinds of preparations and weapons (Tanks,

27) Deedat, Ahmed: *What Is His Name?* Islamic Propagation Centre, Durban, (1986) p. 13.
28) Deedat, A. Op cit p. 14.

> missiles, artillery, aero planes (air force),
> naval ships (navy) etc, and the training of the
> soldiers in these weapons) are all included
> under (the meaning) of the word "force"
> (i.e. land force, navy and air force)...[29]

In a way, Khomeini, Deedat, and bin Hamid are right. How can Islam spread otherwise? What message of salvation do they have to offer convincingly to a sinning world?

Another alternative is to use their oil money to build several multi-million dollar mosques to give the impression that Islam is spreading everywhere. The policy is: Let there be mosques everywhere, even if there are no people to occupy them yet.

In only five years (1985-1990), Muslims have erected 5,002 mosques in Ethiopia alone. In 1945, only one mosque was to be found in the whole of U.K. By 1990, over 1,000 mosques are scattered all over the country. In 1974, there was only one mosque in France. Today, there are over 1,700.

Even though Muslims openly claim to serve the same God as Christians, in reality, they see Christianity as the greatest threat to the incursion of Islam in any land. Despite the apostasy in the Western world, Muslims are aware that Christianity is still growing at an alarming rate.

Thousands are being converted to the Christian faith every year in the free world, and ironically, millions in Communist China. A 1988 survey by *Newsweek* magazine shows Latin

---

29) Hamid, *The Call to Jihad,* p. 20. The Sheikh is a Sunni, not a Shiite. This is necessary because some say only Shiites teach and practice violence.

Americans coming to Christ *en masse* every week. How can the Christian activities be countered by Muslims?

Apart from proliferating mosques, one alternative, especially in Africa, is to entice nominal Christian girls with money, stockfish, jobs, and marry them and convert them to Islam. Muslim youths who marry Christian girls are rewarded. In Europe and America, the goal is to marry the ladies in order to acquire the green card.

They now begin to regard such a country as "our country" and begin to claim the rights they cannot claim in any Islamic land. In Africa, huge sums of money are offered to people to convert them to Islam. A report from a friend in Tanzania says:

> It's common knowledge in our area (of Tanzania) that you can gain a TSH 25,000 reward for winning over a Christian to become a Muslim, and TSH 100,000 if you succeed to convert a pastor or priest to Islam."[30]

An alternative for multiplying is to marry several wives and breed more Muslim children to overpopulate the world and then claim "Islam is the fastest growing religion in the world." According to a U.N. report, the world population in the 90s was growing at the rate of three babies per second (and Muslims have a fair share of this).

While an American or European will have one wife and

---

30) Quoted in Gerhard, Nehls. *Who Cares!? - Our Challenge - Our Chance*. Nairobi: Life Challenge (Africa), 1992, Introduction page.

one or two children, it is estimated that the Islamic world produces 25 million babies annually. That is a way of Islamizing the world! Biological evangelization! And this must never be underestimated.

Muslims are confident that, with the liberal immigration laws for people coming from the Islamic world into the U.S.A., Europe, the U.K. and Australia, they will soon be in the majority and a strong force to be reckoned with, even politically. It is our capitalist greed that is destroying us — the greed of accepting anyone who has money to bring into our economy. The huge investment of Arab petro dollars is enslaving the West.

Islamic authorities also woo the poor African nations with oil money and initiate them into the Organization of Islamic Conferences (O.I.C.). It is a simple principle: He that controls your stomach controls your life.

Many African countries like Togo, with a Muslim population of less than ten percent, are members of the O.I.C. Any member nation has a responsibility to prevent or restrict Christian mission works in their country.

MORE MUSLIMS ARE ABONDONING THEIR FAITH IN THE ALLAH OF ISLAM

The alternatives metioned above are not bringing the best results. Christianity is spreading everywhere. Muslim youths are turning from what some regard as "empty monotonous religiosity" to something more real and vivacious in Christianity.

In West Africa, many young Muslim ladies are renouncing

their Islamic names. Many consider their marital role and insecurity in Islam and opt for Christianity. Some Imams and great scholars are declaring Jesus as Lord.

Nigerian Christians are facing tense opposition from Islam because of the phenomenal rate at which Muslims are getting converted to the Christian faith. Despite its own problems, the church in Nigeria is an aggressively praying church. This has been the key factor behind the present success of mission and evangelistic works in that country.

The devil is not unaware of this, and he can't simply do nothing. It is not uncommon in Northern Nigeria to hear of "The Reverend Ahmed Abdkadir" or "Pastor Abubakar Yusuf." Nothing can be more annoying to Islamic leaders than this because it shows the person was once a Muslim.

To ensure the victory of Islam, something drastic must be done. How did the religion spread in its early stage? Genuine Muslims must return to the effective Islam of Muhammad.

Who is a real Muslim? Muhammad said, "He that flees (runs away from fighting) is not one of us." Claiming to be a real Muslim but refusing to engage in physical fight is apostasy. In the Preface to bin Hamid's *The Call of Jihad*, Mallam M. Salih exclaims:

> "What an hypocrite of a man who regards
> Jihad as an antiquated duty in Islam."

People who regard themselves as genuine Muslims, some of us ignorantly call fanatics: The Muslim youth organizations and their sponsors, al-Jihad groups in Lebanon, al-Mujahideens of Iran and Afghanistan, the Muslim Brotherhood in Egypt and some other countries, the Muslim Students Societies, the Jamat'ul Nasril Islamiyya (JNI), the Hizbullah, the Hamas, al Qaeda, etc. They must establish the kingdom of God on earth.

Their understanding of the kingdom of God is radically different from that of the Bible. Christ said, "*Blessed are the meek, for they shall inherit the earth*" (Matthew 5:5).

Islam says, "No, you cannot be meek and inherit the earth; the believer must rise up and overthrow the present government, impose Islam and be in control."

The Qur'an says, "Power belongeth to Allah, His Apostle, and the believers (i.e. Muslims)." It is therefore necessary for the genuine Muslim to cause *fitna* (anarchy, trouble) until a pure kingdom of Allah is established in a land.

That was the spirit of the Revolution that brought Khomeini to power; it is the spirit driving the Muslim Brotherhood in Egypt and the Alawites in Syria. It is the spirit clamoring for imposition of the Sharia legal system all over the world. It is the Islam of Muhammad. And the world must no longer misunderstand their actions.

When Muslims destroyed churches and killed Christians in Kaduna State of Nigeria in 1987, the government set up a panel to investigate the issue. All parties involved in the incident were asked to submit memoranda to the panel. The Jama'atu Nasril Islamiyya (JNI) said:

> …It is very often found that people who are ignorant of Islam and Muslims have

wrong impressions of the Muslims. Such
ignorant Christians give Muslims all sorts
of bad names such as "fundamentalists,"
"fanatics," etc. as a quality for any faithful
Muslims who believe in living according to
Islamic injunctions. Muslims who are not
serious about their religion are regarded as
progressive. If the Christians knew Islam
well, they would not waste their time trying
to stand in their way as they would realize
that nothing could stand in the way of the
real faithful Muslims.[31]

We understand the irony and undertone here. These are
genuine Muslims. Christians have been ignorant of what
faithful Muslims are supposed to be, and we have suffered
greatly for such ignorance.

It has become a tradition during Muslim festival peri-
ods for many religious and political leaders (including the
popes) to send messages to Muslims to follow the example of
Muhammad and obey Allah, and have religious tolerance.

Either these leaders are yet to know what Islam is, or they
are just saying something to make news. It is impossible to
follow Muhammad's examples in the *Hadiths* and obey his
Allah in the Qur'an and be peaceful, tolerant and submissive
to a government that is not entirely Islamic.

Even in a country like Egypt, where all the key leaders
are Muslims, there will still be unrest by Muslims until a pure

31) Section 4, subsection (C) of its own memorandum.

Islamic government is established and imposed on everyone. As long as Coptic Christians remain in the land and their churches are still visible, Muslims will never rest.

In September 1981, Egyptian Muslims went on an onslaught against the Copts and left 50 dead. Because of this, then President, "Anwar Sadat ordered a wave of arrests and trials of fundamentalists. A month later, an underground Islamic group assassinated him."[32]

Hosni Mubarak, who is trying to present himself as a strict upholder of Islamic values to pacify the Jihadists, has discovered the futility of such thinking. The militants are trying to destroy his rule and establish a pure Islamic rule in the land. To this end, tourism, the mainstay of the Egyptian economy, is being disrupted by attacking Western tourists visiting the historical monuments in Upper Egypt.

There is, simply, no political message that can change a genuine Muslim. What a Muslim needs is a spirit-surgical operation, an operation done by the Holy Spirit of God, a spiritual heart transplant, a transplantation of a new nature. That is why salvation is known as a regeneration. It is what Jesus calls being born again (John 3:3).

At Christmas and Easter times, our leaders also make their traditional messages to Christians to be peaceful. But Christians do not need a politician to tell them to be peaceful. Our God teaches us not only to *follow peace with all men,*" but also to *"turn the other cheek"* even in the face of provocation.

---

32) *The Middle East* magazine, London: June 1992, p. 23.

> But I say unto you which hear, Love your
> enemies, do good to them which hate you,
> Bless them that curse you, and pray for them
> which despitefully use you. And unto him
> that smiteth thee on the one cheek offer
> also the other.[33]

That sounds outlandish, but is the teaching of our Saviour. No religion can preach that. Jesus demonstrated this by laying down His life so that those who believe Him might have eternal life. He is our Shepherd and we are His sheep. He fights on our behalf. We do not need a politician to tell us that.

Many of our leaders condone or even promote Islam and yet tell Muslims to be peaceful. Until a Muslim is born again, he can hardly be peaceful. To imagine a real Qur'an-practicing, *Hadith*-obeying peaceful Muslim is like imagining a weightless stone, a round square or an elastic glass. As we have seen in the Qur'an, Allah says:

> Fight against those who (1) believe not
> in Allah, (2) nor in the Last Day, (3) nor
> forbid that which has been forbidden by
> Allah and His Messenger (4) and those who
> acknowledge not the religion of truth (i.e.
> Islam) among the people of the Scripture
> (Jews and Christians), until they pay the
> Jizyah…[34]

If, by believing and practicing the gospel of Jesus Christ,

33) Luke 6:27-28.
34) Sura 9:29 (Hilali and Khan).

one becomes the enemy of Allah, who is *this* Allah that is so offended by the gospel of Christ? Can he be the God of the Bible who singled out Jesus in the midst of the two greatest prophets of the Bible, and then marked Him out, declaring "*This is **my beloved Son**: hear him?*" (Luke 9:35). If by "hearing Him" we offend someone named Allah, don't we have good reasons to research the identity of this Allah?

> "*Send missionaries to Burundi, Zaire, Uganda... to combat the evil activities of Christian missionaries there,*" said Muammar Ghaddafi of Libya to fellow Muslims. "*God wants you to fight in one rank and he who does not do this is outside Islam and God will not let him enter paradise....*"[35]

In a prophetic utterance, the Lord Jesus said concerning the Christians: "*...the time cometh, that whosoever killeth you will think that he doeth God service.*" The Lord quickly added, "*And these things will they do unto you, because they have not known the Father, nor me.*"[36]

This simply means that the Allah our killers claim to know as God may not be the real Father. This is why we have to take the pains and patience to find out who this Allah is that stirs them against us. Such a venture is necessary for the church and government.

NIGERIA EXPERIENCES ISLAMIC TERRORISM

As Islam was practiced by Muhammad, so it is today. No

35) Nigerian *Sunday Punch*, Lagos: January 26, 1986.
36) John 16:2-3.

extremism. In fact, there is less carnage today than then. This is obviously because there are civil and criminal laws that handicap any savage behavior in the name of religion.

Nigeria has seen practical Islam. There are too many cases to cite. Here are a few from the past twenty years.

During the 1980 Maitatsine Islamic uproar in Kano, 4,177 people were reported (officially) slaughtered with property worth millions of dollars destroyed. Two years later, on October 30, 1982, eight big churches were burned in Kano.

That same year the Muslims struck in Kaduna and 400 people were officially reported as killed. In October of the same year, members of the Muslim Students Society (MSS) struck in Sabon Gari in Kano and killed two people. (Many of those killed were not just Christians but also people of different sects in the same religion of Islam).

In 1984, Muslims in Yola and Jimeta went berserk and killed 700, including policemen. 5,913 people were rendered homeless. They also besieged Gombe and more than 100 people were killed.[37]

On May 3, 1986, the Muslim students of the then University of Sokoto went on a rampage attacking other students of the University with dangerous weapons. While these Muslim students were still boiling in Sokoto, their counterparts in Ibadan were setting fire to the sculpture of Jesus in the Chapel of the Resurrection at the University of Ibadan.

The following year, March 6, 1987, at the College of

37) Lagos: *Time International*, March 19, 1984, p. 6.

Education, Kafanchan in Kaduna State, Muslims went on a rampage they expected would spread to the South. This engulfed Kafanchan, Kaduna and Zaria. Of the 150 churches in Zaria city alone, only one escaped being burned down in three days of Jihad.

Many Christians were slain in cold blood while some were burned alive. Many homes belonging to Christians and cars with Christian stickers were burned in all these cities.

This writer traveled to Kaduna and Zaria in Nigeria to see things for himself. The cause of the riot: A female Muslim college student accused the Reverend Abubakar Bako (a former Muslim) of "misinterpreting" the Qur'an in his preaching.

Muslims believe that no non-Muslim should quote the Qur'an on any issue because he cannot understand it. However, a Muslim can quote the Bible to prove that Jesus is not the Son of God.

The Chaplain of the Ahmadu Bello University, Dr. Ben Oruma, whose ministry in the Chapel has helped depopulate the Muslim students in the university, was one of their main targets. From his house, he was pursued several miles. Finally, they beat him and slashed his body with machetes.

"They thought they had finished me," said Dr. Oruma, "As they were leaving, I faintly heard them chanting 'Allahu Akbar, Allahu Akbar" (i.e. Allah is greater, Allah is greater than all)... for handing over his enemy into their hands."

It would be impossible to list all the atrocities being perpetrated in Nigeria alone by Muslims since the Uthman

Dan Fodio Jihad that engulfed that country in 1804. Yet all these must never be taken as extremism. Violence in Islam is both a doctrine and a person.

In Christianity, peace is both a teaching to obey and a Person to possess. When one is possessed with either of these "persons," one can't help behaving accordingly. The seemingly most peaceful among Muslims have proven this to us. But they have killed us only to embolden us. Our voice is louder at death than in life. Thousands of Christians have been slaughtered; but Muslims know they can never succeed in silencing us.

We will not wait for Islam to stifle us and enslave our free nations as they did in North Africa, and many other places in the world, where it has become an offense to openly confess the Christian faith or convert a person to Christianity.

As merciful as our God is, He never forgives those who do not acknowledge their sins and repent. For all the violence Muslims have done to Christians, they have not repented and they must not think they can continue in such savagery unchecked.

In 1991 and 1992 there were three more riots by Nigerian Muslims in Katsina, Bauchi and Kano cities during which thousands lost their lives. In Bauchi, the immediate cause was the sale of what a Muslim believed to be roasted pork by a Christian in Tafawa Balewa area (a Christian area) which the Muslim bought and allegedly ate.

For allegedly "tempting" the Muslim, the meat seller was commanded to be killed. Hundreds of souls died from both sides. That means if a Muslim mistakenly eats bacon in a restaurant in America or Europe, the Islamic community may set the restaurant ablaze and the attendants may be slaughtered!

In Kano, the Muslims were rioting to protest a proposed Christian evangelistic program by German preacher, Reinhard Bonnke. Many unprintable atrocities were reported. Evangelist Reinhard Bonnke had just been in two Islamic cities, Kaduna and Ilorin, and hundreds of thousands of Muslims were converted to Christ and God did many spectacular miracles. Many crutches and turbans were left on the floor at the end of each night's program.

Now a similar one was to be held in the ancient Islamic city of Kano. Muslims felt this was dangerous to their faith. Their swords were continuously busy for several days, slaughtering Christians.

Two members of our ministry were in Kano right after the riot. They heard how some jihadists reportedly dragged a pregnant woman out of a hospital, slashed her womb with dagger and flung out "the infidel thing inside her!" Nigerian *National Concord* (October 28, 1991), a newspaper owned by a Muslim, reported:

> They (the Muslims) were armed with machetes, daggers, swords and other dangerous weapons killing Christians at random and setting their houses and shops ablaze.

Eye witnesses" reports say: "A Christian

man got delivered from an untimely death through the sound of a fire brigade siren. The vandals decided to torture this man to death. First, they felt there was no reason for him to have two hands, yet they all had two each, hence his right hand was cut off immediately. They were thrilled by his dance of agony; therefore they went ahead to cut off the other one. As they were about to pick on the other appendages, suddenly came the blaring of the fire brigade siren which they mistook for the police, hence they took to their heels, thereby abandoning their victim…

…In one of the refugee camps, a pregnant woman forcefully gave birth to a baby prematurely while the pastor of a devoted Bible believing church died shortly after escaping into one of the camps,… perhaps scared by the horrors unleashed against fellow brethren.

…A Christian lady (Sister Bridget) who hailed from the eastern part of Nigeria lost all her four children and watched her husband helplessly stabbed to death.

…As the next day (October 15, 1991) brightened up, so the sun of persecution rose again… One of the victims of this Tuesday was one Mr. Samuel who hailed from Benue State. He was beaten to a state of coma before they pounced on his family. His wife and children were treated very inhumanly. Daggers were inserted into their throats and after shouting "Allahu Akbar" and a few other Arabic words, mother and children were slaughtered like ileya (sacrifice) rams...

...Pastor Friday Akpan, the vicar of Christ Faith Church, Kano, was beaten mercilessly and his head virtually in pieces like a coconut by Muslim arsonists. Thereafter, they burnt the church he pastored...

...An Ibo woman, seven months pregnant, was killed while about eight people were locked up in a room and set ablaze. Some other people numbering about twelve were thrown inside a deep open well and the well was securely locked up.

But the highest degree of callousness displayed was when a young lady in her twenties was slaughtered, having her breasts cut off and thrown away, while her private part was also cut off and placed in her mouth. As of Wednesday, her corpse was (still) lying at Murtala Muhammad Hospital...

If you could recite the "Kalimat Shahad," (La illaha il Allah etc, an indication that you were a Moslem, you would be spared.

If not, you would be quickly sacrificed at
the altar of Allah.[38]

A team of the Nigerian *Newswatch* magazine reporters
who went to cover the butchery wrote that it would be against
decency to publish some of the pictures they took in Kano.
In Dublin, this author saw one of the photographs of these
Nigerian Jihads in which three young Muslim men held
down a Christian lady while one of them beheaded her.

We easily forget history, and thus put our generation and
posterity in danger. An Elder of the Evangelical Church of
West Africa (ECWA), in Kaduna was burned to death with
his church during the 1987 riots. This church was rebuilt
at the cost of about $10,000.

In May 1992, while a Christian stage play going on in
this same church, a band of Muslims set it on fire again, killing at least 20 people inside. The Assistant Secretary of the
church, Musa Bakut, was not there, but the Muslims went
to his house and slaughtered him and his son, burned his
car and left the wife half dead. They did not kill her because
they suddenly remembered that Muhammad said they should
not kill women or children during any jihad.[39]

THE ISLAMIC PHILOSOPHY OF PEACE

Have you ever heard that Islam is a religion of peace?
Islam, indeed, is a religion of "peace." But we must understand what "peace" means in Islam.

38) *Acts of Apostles Continued* by Ed Mitchell. New Mexico (USA): Josiah
Publishing.
39) *Today's Challenge* magazine, Nos. 3 & 4, 1992. Jos: ECWA Productions
Ltd., P.M.B. 2010, Jos, Nigeria.

This is best illustrated in a Jewish ballad that tells of a sardine swimming off the shores of Eilat. The fish meets a shark and humbly says the normal greeting, *shalom!* (peace). To avoid a clash, the sardine gives up his tails, some fins, some scales, but all these avail nothing. For a real and lasting peace, he surrenders everything. The shark nods in agreement and utters the word "peace," opens his mouth and swallows the sardine whole. That is the lasting "peace."

In government offices in Northern Nigeria, the Christian's fins, tail and scales have been chopped off by his Muslim boss. His schools (where the Muslim big man was also educated), as well as his hospitals, have been taken over and given Islamic names. But all this is not the lasting peace.

In Islam, "peace" is not achieved until Islam has swallowed the nation. Peace means total eradication of their enemies. It means subjugating, killing or swallowing all non-conformists. Nobody should ever imagine "giving peace a chance" in a nation with a significant number of Muslims. If America does not learn this, she must be ready to suffer more.

As Richard Wurmbrand has said, Christians are not going to quarrel, but we are not going to allow any shark to swallow us either.

> "Children of God are too valuable a species; we have to survive… while we must loathe war, we also had to defeat Hitler, the lover of war."[40]

Late in 1989, key Muslim leaders from all over Africa

---

40) Wurmbrand, Richard. *A Hundred Meditations*, p. 142.

gathered in Nigeria. One of the resolutions: "Islam in Africa Organization" (IAO) founded, and Nigeria made its "permanent headquarters." Members concluded:

> "We are ready to go to any length to get
> Sharia established in this country (Nigeria)
> whether we are alive or dead." [41]

Should Christians be silent so we do not provoke a riot? Muslims do not need to be provoked. For them, it does not take two to fight. If they have to obey the injunctions of Allah in the Qur'an and follow Muhammad's examples and instructions in the *Hadith*, they do not have to be provoked.

Genuine Muslims are always meditating on what next to do to "convert" the enemies of Allah. For them, everybody must be judged by Sharia, the law of Allah.

Nigeria is to Africa what Britain and America are to the Western world. Islamic leaders believe if they can win Nigeria, they will win all of Africa.

When the International Islamic Conference was held in Britain in 1976, Muslims vowed, "If we can win London for Islam, it won't be hard to win the whole Western world."[42]

Many English people could not imagine Muslims realizing such an aspiration. But Islam has made great progress in Britain, with over 1000 mosques already. Because of centuries of unrest in the Islamic world, many Muslims are disenchanted and fleeing *en masse* to the West.

However, instead of presenting the gospel to them, we

---

41) *Daily Sketch,* Ibadan, December 14, 1989, p. 8.
42) *Battle Cry,* Chick Publications, California, Sept/Oct, 1990.

are allowing them to establish mosques and Islamic centers and continue their religion. Birmingham, Coventry and Manchester are being filled with Muslims from the Middle East, Pakistan, India, etc. The University of Birmingham has been "colonized" by Muslim students.

In 2005, the student union government of the university "banned" the Christian Union of the university and froze their account. Their contention: the Christian body refused to amend their constitution to allow non-Christian students to be elected to the Christian Union leadership. To them, this was discrimination.

They have no respect for the religion and culture of their hosts. Where they have a foothold, they build royal castles and become kings. We may think we are helping them but we are not. Nor are we helping ourselves and the next generation.

Instead of these people beginning a new and quiet life in the free world, they are making much noise for an Islamic Parliament. Their clamor has been influencing the British lawmakers in many areas, especially concerning the status of Christianity and Islam in the land. Muslims are also calling for laws in Britain to amputate the hands of thieves as is done in Islamic countries, making *Sharia* operative in the Western world.

If Muslims are convinced that their god must rule us in the free world, they have to wait and let us first study that god and his manifestoes and Constitution thoroughly; for the Bible says: *"Blessed is the nation whose God is THE LORD."*

If the Muslim god is the Allah of the Islamic strongholds of the world, where one cannot speak of freedom or fundamental human rights; if he is the god of Kuwait, where a woman cannot vote, or the god of Saudi, where a woman must not drive a car, or the god of Iran, where a wife has to get an "exit permit" from her husband before leaving the house; if he is the inspirer of Muhammad and the speaker in the Qur'an, we in the free world need to study him to determine if we should allow him to rule our land.

The Western world, especially Britain, America, Australia and the Netherlands, have an illusion of being fair to all, not wanting to annoy Muslims.

The Australian and British parliaments are even trying to make a law against speaking anything against other people's religion. After the September 11 attack on the U.S., President Bush gave a similar warning in order to convince Muslims that the war he was mobilizing against terrorism was not a war against Islam.

We respect our political leaders. But we regard this particular attitude as hypocrisy because many things are said and written against Biblical Christianity by the press all over the world, and particularly by Muslim writers, yet none of these lawmakers objects.

In the past few years, a number of Pakistani Christians have been sentenced to death for "blasphemy against the sacred name of the Holy Prophet Muhammad." Yet the West has not considered such governments as evil because they have not attacked America.

Turkey has a legislation prohibiting "insulting the books, prophets, or values of another religion." Turkish government though, theoretically secular, is Islamic. Under this law, a Christian was arrested and charged in February 2001 with "blaspheming" the Qur'an and Muhammad. But this law has never been used to charge any Muslim despite all the anti-Christian books and sermons of Turkish Muslims.

People do not realize that even the Qur'an insults Jesus. It repudiates and undermines the authority of the Bible. To say that Jesus is not the Son of God, for example, is blasphemous. If a Christian writes that Muhammad is not a prophet of God, this is highly blasphemous and offensive to a Muslim government. But in every sermon and prayer session of a Muslim, the deity of Jesus and the Holy Spirit must be denied. This is done by the compulsory recitation of Sura 112.

The aim of Islam is to engulf the world. As a matter of policy, Muslims do not want to be "offended" or "assaulted;" but they can go to any length to assault other religions, especially Christianity. In Islamic countries, it is lawful for a Muslim to convert a Christian to Islam, but illegal, in fact, a serious crime for a Christian to attempt to convert a Muslim to Christianity. In some of these countries, the Christian preacher may face the death penalty.

Muslims believe they must claim a right to build mosques everywhere in Europe and America while it is legally unimaginable to allow churches in their own countries. It is a pretension of liberality for our lawmakers to take lightly the Islamic threats and terrorism in the West. As we take the attitude of "live and let live" towards Islam, it will surely live; but it will live to destroy us!

THE RIGHT TO WEEP ALOUD

Where Islam gets a foothold, it becomes a stronghold. It persecutes Christians and makes all attempts to silence the church. It can wound and take away the right of the victim to cry.

The Coptic Christians in Egypt have suffered continued persecution for centuries, and they are still under the same oppression of Muslims. In the last two decades, so many Christians have been slaughtered in Nigeria that religious riots there are no longer newsworthy. In recent riots, Christians have tried to retaliate and defend themselves, and this has been very bloody.

If Muslims had no basis in the Qur'an and the *Hadith* for their violence, we would regard them as extremists. That is one of the reasons why we have to study the god that is speaking in the Qur'an and that has been inspiring them against us.

This millennium is very crucial in God's program and also in the agenda of the devil. Many attempts are being made to close doors to Christian mission works in many nations. But we are confident that now is the time that many of the captives of Islam in many seemingly impenetrable Islamic countries will be set free by the power of the Holy Spirit. They may chain some of us but they cannot chain the Word of God. They may ban us from entering their countries, but they cannot ban the Holy Spirit of God from penetrating and convicting their captives.

By faith and by the power of the Holy Spirit we will create wings on the Word of God to fly into nations and into the hearts of men. Through satellites, we will beam the Gospel into the bedrooms of chief Imams. Their youth shall be delivered; their old monarchs shall be saved.

All Islamic countries are in God's program. They must all be represented in heaven (Revelation 7:9-10). But after the victory of Jesus for their salvation two thousand years ago, the enemy of their souls is still holding them in bondage of false religion and demonic influences.

Billions have died in their sins and in a false hope. But by His sovereignty and because of His love, God is going to reach out to all these nations to save some by all means. It is impossible for any security device, or for persecution or terrorism to prevent this. God is going to show Himself sovereign in these nations.

Jesus said: *"Go ye therefore, and teach* (or make disciples of) *all nations…"* (Matthew 28:19). God is already giving us the necessary enduement and the required equipment to get the job done, and nothing can stop us.

Speaking of rescuing religiously enslaved people, Jesus said that no man can *"enter a strongman's house, and spoil his goods, except he first bind the strong man."* (Matthew 12:29). By the power of the Lord, we are penetrating into the strongman's bases to release his captives.

AN OPEN CHALLENGE

Many Muslims believe they must fight Christianity and Western civilization. But Muslims don't need to fight. Jesus said, "*I am the Way,* **the Truth,** *and the Life*" (John 14:6) The religious leaders of His days said, No. They crucified Him. But on the third day, He rose again, appeared to many in Jerusalem for forty days before ascending to heaven. He is still alive today in His majestic glory.

This is to demonstrate that TRUTH has an inherent ability of defense and survival. As Christians, we have never been moved by the provocative blasphemous Islamic pamphlets, audio and videocassettes circulating all over the world. We do not believe we must shed blood to defend the truth. Ultimately, truth is always victorious.

Muslims, however, want to defend Islam by any imaginable means. But if the religion of Muhammad is "the Truth" or even a truth of the Truth, Allah need not command Muslims to use physical swords to preserve it. Jesus was crucified by fire-breathing Roman soldiers, yet He rose up again. The Islamic truth should be able to resurrect if crucified. Let Muslims, therefore, relax and see what the printing press can do in crucifying their "truth."

Who is afraid of the pen and the press? The truth of the Christian faith has undergone pen crucifixion for several centuries, yet it is still alive, spreading everywhere without the force of arms. Never does a single day pass when no one is converted to the Bible truth.

It is only in countries with Christian orientation and influence that a man is free to think and believe as he likes. It is an offense to be a citizen of an Islamic country and believe and preach that Jesus is the Saviour.

Christian literature and missionaries are not allowed. Why? If what you believe is false, you need force to keep people in it. If Muslims believe their "truth" is invulnerable, let the Islamic world open its gates to the Bible, Christian literature and to men and women, anointed and sent by the Holy Ghost, and let us see for the next decade what "the Sword of the Spirit" can do in a free environment. Let us see what the anointing can do in breaking the yoke of falsehood. This is the open challenge!

Even though Muslims write many things to attack the Christian faith, they are afraid of a Christian approaching the Qur'an with a critical knife. We know that real truth is never afraid of a lie. A lie fears the truth. That is why Christians allow the mind to exercise itself to grasp the truth and then decide. No coercion. Once one experiences the truth, one will never be afraid of a lie but simply deride it.

This writer has read several books by agnostics, atheists, humanists, psychologists, communists and Muslim scholars. But an average Muslim is afraid of Christian literature, especially on Islam. He is afraid he may be confronted with some facts that may scatter his faith in Islam. He is even ready to slay the writer. Why? Because he wants to defend "the truth." But truth, by its virtue, is able to defend itself.

Moreover, a real truth is not worth killing for boldly, but is worth dying for willingly. A religion that is not worth dying for is not worth living for. Yet a religious man must be sure he is not dying for a lie or deception. Why would some brilliant young men be instructed to hijack and crash airplanes and get roasted in them in order to destroy the perceived enemies of their religion?

Ironically, the leaders of these young men were hiding in caves in Afghanistan, afraid of dying. Meanwhile, they have convinced their followers that after roasting in a plane, they will open their eyes in Paradise in the bosom of women. A lie is powerful indeed. But five minutes after death is enough to discover the wickedness of an age-long lie.

LET ALLAH CONTEND

We must defend our beliefs against falsehood (by presenting the truth), but we should not kill to defend God's reputation. Christians are commanded to love and pray for their enemies, not kill them." God is well able to execute His own vengeance. The Bible says, "Vengeance is mine; I will repay, saith the Lord" (Romans 12:19).

Late in 1987 a Muslim decided to bulldoze the graves of certain white Christian missionaries at Ibi town in the Wukari Local Government Area of the present Taraba State of Nigeria to extend his estate. God spoke to a Christian to tell the Emir, the Muslim traditional ruler of the town, to warn the man. The Emir was reluctant because of his religious leaning.

On December 24, the graves were bulldozed. Immediately, a mysterious fire started. The bulldozer was the first victim. From the bulldozer, the fire selectively burned the property of several Muslims in that town. Only little children could see the fire approaching any of its targets.

The invisible fire continued from that Christmas Eve

until March the following year. By January, the fire had gutted about 400 houses, according to a report by a Northern Nigerian based secular newspaper, *The Reporter*, of January 30, 1988.

By March, the number of houses affected had grown to about 3,000. Some Muslims who had not been affected and were quick to realize that the fire was selective, went to hide their belongings in the nearby town and villages. But the fire could identify the properties from Ibi town and did justice to those properties, leaving those of their hosts in the same houses intact!

The only Christians who had a brush with the fire were the few who dared sympathize with their Muslim friends:

> A Muslim parent who beat his child for
> joining some Christians in prayer meeting,
> had his house gutted that very evening.[43]

That sounds like a folktale in the 21st century, but it was real. At least two secular newspapers and three Christian publications reported this strange fire. Even the federal government-controlled national TV, Nigerian Television Authority (NTA Lagos) reported it in a program, *Newsline*. The Federal Government set up a committee of seismologists to investigate the cause and extent of the damage of the mysterious fire. The Committee had no scientific explanation.

When all efforts, sacrifices and prayers sought by the Emir failed to stop the fire, it became obvious that the Christian God was defending even the dry bones of His servants who

43) *Good News* magazine, April/May, 1988, Kaduna, Nigeria.

had died as far back as 1904. Even though the Christians realized they must not sympathise with the Muslims, they did not rejoice over what happened. The fire did not hurt any person. It only destroyed their property. God loves the people! He was only teaching them a lesson.

The Christian leaders then summoned the people together and preached the gospel of Jesus Christ to them. A Christian organization, Love Divine Ministry, based in Kaduna, was there. Over 400 people (most of them Muslims) repented and were converted to Christ. Some also said that God had also healed them of physical diseases and disablements.

People serving a great God need not defend Him. A God worth His name is able to defend himself and his followers. Islamic terrorism belittles the Allah of Islam. It does not show the strength of Islam but its fears and weaknesses.

In the Old Testament, when the people of Israel backslid and began to worship Baal, one of them, Gideon, rose up one night and destroyed the altar of Baal, of which his father Joash was the priest:

> And when the men of the city arose early in the morning, behold, the altar of Baal was cast down, and the grove was cut down…! And they said one to another, Who hath done this thing? And when they inquired and asked, they said, Gideon the son of Joash hath done this thing. Then the men of the city said unto Joash, Bring out thy son, that he might die: because he hath cast down the altar of Baal, and because he hath

cut down the grove that was by it.

And Joash said unto all that stood against
him, Will ye plead for Baal? will ye save
him? he that will plead for him, let him be
put to death whilst it is yet morning: if he
be a god, let him plead for himself, because
one hath cast down his altar. Therefore on
that day he called him Jerubaal, saying, Let
Baal plead against him, because he hath
thrown down his altar.[44]

The law of Joash could be made an international law
today: that a nation, or whoever, that promotes or instigates
the killing of a supposed infidel, blasphemer or heretic should
be sanctioned even by military force by other nations, if
necessary. As far as Christians are concerned, *we do not have
to defend our God.*

Muslims claim they can use violence if their god or
prophet is blasphemed. If a person is blaspheming their
god or breaking down the altar of their religion through
pen and paper, why don't they allow Allah to contend with
the blasphemer? That would be the more religious thing to
do. If Allah is a savior, a man should not have to save him
from the hand of an infidel. All we can do is to rename such
a person "Jerub-allah."

A god that weak human beings must fight for cannot be
the Almighty God. We therefore challenge our Muslim friends
all over the world to lay down their swords, bombs and knives,

44) Judges 6:27-32.

matches and gasoline, and let Allah defend himself.

IT'S A SIN TO HELP GOD!

There is the story of Uzzah in the Bible who wanted to help God. The ark of God was being carried on a cart to the City of David amidst 30,000 people singing and dancing:

> And when they came to Nachon's thresh-
> ingfloor, Uzzah put forth his hand to the
> ark of God... for the oxen shook it. And
> the anger of the LORD was kindled against
> Uzzah; and God smote him there because
> of his error; and there he died by the ark
> of God.[45]

Here we see a zealous man who felt that God's reputa-tion was at stake. He thought the Lord who is enthroned between the cherubim in heaven could fall from His throne, so "*Uzzah put forth his hand...* "and received instant judgment. Of course, God was not in the ark, but the ark represented His covenant with Israel and His glory. God can never fall from His throne!

No idolater, no philosopher, no Islamic or non-Islamic writer can fell God. If Muslims think their Allah is indeed God, allow him to defend himself. If Allah is God and Mus-lims are defending his reputation, they must know that they are incurring the wrath of God upon themselves. It is like saying, "Allah is helpless and I must do something or his reputation will crumble." That would be irreverent!

45) 2 Samuel 6:1-11.

AMERICA BREEDS ISLAMIC TERRORISM

CHAPTER THREE

WE CHERISH our freedom and democracy. But a country that allows any popular social or religious evil in the name of freedom is a demon-craze. The USA and the American church welcomes Islam and give it full expression.

Not only are Muslims free to fill America with mosques, even a Baptist University, Shaw University, in North Carolina has a mosque in honor of the Saudi King, Khalid Ben Abdul Aziz Al-Saud.

This is a dangerously hypocritical pretension of democracy and hospitality. No church is allowed in the Saudi kingdom, much less on an Islamic university campus.

As a democracy, we cannot prevent Muslims from believing whatever they want to believe. But any belief that is injurious to our own freedom and wellbeing must be checked.

The United States Congress adopted a resolution in 1980 to congratulate Islam for its 14 centuries of existence. The Congress pledged its support for Islam and promised to promote the understanding of Islam in America.

At the same time, the U.S. National Council of Churches, presenting itself as the voice of Christians in the United States, sent a congratulatory message to all Muslim organizations in America on this 14th century anniversary of Islam.

Immediately after this anniversary and the pledge for support that Islamic leaders received from the government and "the church," Islam began to grow in the U.S. Many more Muslims began flooding America to study and to settle down. They had feared that if they went to America they would be converted to Christianity. But that fear was removed.

Some of these Islamic organizations that the Council of Churches congratulated are now blacklisted today as behind some of the terrorist problems America is facing.

Want more? Wallace Deen Muhammad, son of the founder of the Nation of Islam or Black Muslims, Elijah Muhammad, was invited by the U.S. Senate to give the opening prayer at the Senate. The assumption was that the Allah the Black Muslim leader would invoke was the same God that any Christian leader would pray to. If the Allah that the Senate invited at its opening session was not God, the Senate put itself in trouble.

America allied with Saudi Arabia Islamic fighters in billions of dollars worth of arms and ammunition to support the *mujahideen*, the Islamic "freedom fighters" of Afghanistan to resist Russia. Russia lost the war with great casualties. The arms America "donated" were used to establish the anti-Christian Taliban regime that eventually aimed at destroying the Western civilization and became an avowed enemy of the Gospel.

When Afghanistan was resisting Russian invasion, it made it clear it was fighting a jihad. They believed it was a religious war of protecting Islam. As far as they were concerned, America had joined them to fight a jihad. Later, when they also attacked America, they believed it was a continuation of their jihad. But America remained ignorant.

CIA boss William Casey persuaded the US Congress to support the Islamic fighters of Pakistan and Afghanistan in their resistance of the Communist incursion. America eventually gave hundreds of Stinger anti-aircraft missiles to shoot down Soviet planes. The American government also sent war advisers to train the Islamic fighters.

The CIA also joined the Saudi and Pakistani intelligence agencies to recruit radical Muslims to come to Pakistan from all over the world to fight with the "freedom fighters."

Within ten years, about 35,000 Muslim volunteers from 43 Islamic countries in the Middle East, Africa, Central Asia and the Far East had joined the training. Many Islamic centers were established by the Pakistani Islamic military government to help in this training. Altogether, about 100,000 Muslims underwent these training programs.

The training camps became Islamic war colleges for future Islamic radicalism. Did the American intelligence agencies ever consider the consequences of bringing together these thousands of Islamic radicals from all over the world?

Among these thousands of foreign Islamic fighters and trainees was a young Saudi student, Osama bin Laden, the son of a Yemeni construction businessman, Muhammad bin Laden, a close friend of the late King Faisal. Osama is the 17th of the 57 children by his father and a Saudi mother.

Osama's enormous wealth first came from his father's company, which was given contracts by the Saudi King to renovate and expand the mosques in Mecca and Medina. He used this wealth to sponsor the training and fighting in Afghanistan and Pakistan. He later settled down there to oversee the work.

Donations for these fighters also came from the Saudi Intelligence, the Saudi Red Crescent (the Islamic version of the Red Cross Society), the World Muslim League and private donations from Saudi princes and mosques.

After the September 11 attack, former CIA Director, R. James Woolsey confirmed that much of the money for *Al Qaeda* had come from Saudi Arabia. Support also came from drug (marijuana) smuggling that the *mujahideen* were involved in across the Pakistani borders.

The recruiting and training of these jihadists was done initially to resist Communism. But by the time the war against Russia ended, the militant organizations and networks could not be disbanded. They formulated a goal to promote and defend Islam against all non-Muslim governments all over the world. They had all the training and expertise needed as well as some intelligence and military facilities.

About 500 US-made anti-aircraft missiles donated to the fighters remained with them after the war with Russia. These were the weapons the Taliban used to shoot down American helicopters in the October 2001 war on terrorism.

In 1986, Osama bin Laden used his wealth and construction equipment to build the Khost tunnel complex near the Pakistani border. This is a major arms depot under the mountains, with training and medical facilities for the Islamic fighters.

Pakistani journalist, Ahmed Rashid, a member of the International Consortium of Investigative Journalists, and correspondent for *The Daily Telegraph* of London, says the Khost project was co-funded by the CIA.

Osama eventually became a figure to be reckoned with as he set up *al-Qaeda* (The Base), which now controls a networ of Islamic militant organizations worldwide.

When the US-led allied forces came to Saudi Ara a base for the Gulf War against Iraq, this upset Os Laden and he openly declared war on these Ame British infidels. His case: Allah's land was too the infidels. It was a desecration of the holy s American and British soils are not too un children to come and live there).

America did not take Osama serious these Afghanistan-Pakistani trained Is the World Trade Center in New Yor wounding about a thousand.

1) http://
5753C1A9
2) Sura 5:5

Osama went to Somalia and mobilized his members to kill 18 US soldiers in October of that same year. Yet it was not until 1997 that the CIA began to see Osama as a real threat and created a cell to monitor his activities.

In February 1998, Osama bin Laden, with other radicals, issued a "*fatwa,*" an Islamic religious decree, saying:

> "The killing of Americans and their civilian and military allies is a religious duty for each and every Muslim to be carried out in whichever country they are..."[1]

It wasn't an empty threat. Many Americans have been killed since. After the September 11, 2001 attack, killing about 3,000 people, the US Congress approved an enormous sum of $40 billion to fight Osama and his network of "freedom fighters." That is part of the cost of spiritual ignorance. We must learn that it is cheaper to prevent evil than to combat it. But it is still doubtful that America has really learned her lessons.

Israel and Christianity are the avowed enemies of Islam, and the Qur'an makes no pretension about this:

> Take not the Jews and the Christians as friends, they are but friends to one another. And if any amongst you takes them (as friends) then surely he is one of them. Verily, Allah guides not those people who are unjust.[2]

ery.nytimes.com/gst/fullpage.html?res=9406EEDC173CF936A3
79C8B63
   (Hilali and Khan).

This is not Osama bin Laden. This is Allah talking. Any acrimony the Islamic world has for the Jews is transferred to any people or nation that befriends the Jews. That is the major "sin" of America. Because she is perceived as the bastion of Christianity and the greatest friend of the Jews, she has to be attacked.

The real enemy is not America. They believe if America is weakened, Israel will be crushed. Moreover, if America's strength is destroyed, it will be easy to exterminate Christianity in both the Islamic world, and in the Western world. That is why America and Israel have been the targets of Islamic international terrorism for the past twenty years. Let us realize that Allah had already said this before the present Palestinian problems started.

In 1983, a car bomb destroyed the Israeli Embassy in Argentina. In April 1983, a suicide bomber destroyed the U.S. Embassy in Beirut, Lebanon, killing 63 people. In October of the same year, the U.S. marine barracks in Beirut was attacked and 299 perished. In September 1987, a UTA passenger flight over the Muslim country of Chad was destroyed with 170 passengers and crew.

In December 1988, a Pan Am flight over Lockerbie was bombed, leaving 270 dead. Fingers pointed at some people whom the Muslim terrorist Moamar Ghaddafi of Libya defended and protected.

On March 17, 1992, a car bomb destroyed the Israeli Embassy in Argentina, killing 29 people and injuring 242. Five months later, Islamic militants in Algeria exploded a bomb at the Algiers airport and killed 12, leaving 128 injured.

One year later, the terrorists exploded a massive bomb below the World Trade Center, New York City.

In July 1994, a Jewish Center in the Argentine capital was attacked, killing 96 people. Three months after, 23 people perished in Tel Aviv, Israel when a suicide bomb exploded.

On June 25, 1996, a fuel truck carrying a bomb exploded outside a U.S. military housing facility in Dhahran in Saudi Arabia and 19 people were destroyed with 515 others badly burnt. The anti-US Islamic groups claimed responsibility.

In 1998 the American embassies in Kenya and Tanzania were bombed on the same day, August 7th. 224 people perished and 5,500 others were injured.

In October 2000, Islamic suicide militants bombed the American warship in Yemen and killed 17.

Then came the most fatal attack so far: Over 3,000 men, women and children were crushed and burned to death when two passenger planes were used as missiles to destroy the World Trade Center in New York. Another plane heavily damaged the Pentagon.

While the world stood aghast and America was mourning, many Muslims were dancing and jubilating in many parts of the world. Three days after this attack, Muslims in the Christian city of Jos in Northern Nigeria left their Friday worship with knives, bows and arrows and killed Christians and burned churches. No less than 500 people died.

Three weeks after the September 11 attack on America, a plane full of Jews crashed into the Black Sea. Fingers pointed at the anti-Israeli Islamic terrorists.

About a week later, some Muslims in Kano, Nigeria, left their Friday worship with weapons of war and started slaughtering Christians in that city.

Two days later, their counterparts in Pakistan entered a church and killed as many worshippers as they could because they knew some Americans were there.

Reasonable people believe the September 11 attack on America was Islamic. The Federal Bureau of Investigation (FBI) discovered a letter left by some of the hijackers.

The translation is by a professional Arab American translator, Radman Hakim, and was published by the *Los Angeles Times*. Where Hakim used the term "God," I used "Allah." This, as I pointed out, is because the Arabic text does not have the word "Ilah" (i.e. "God") but "Allah."

I have quoted the whole letter but tried to draw attention to some statements by italicizing them. What to do at every stage is described to their last minute in the plane:

The Final Night

1) Renewing your covenant with Allah.

2) Know all aspects of the plan very well and expect the reaction and the resistance from the enemy.

3) Read the Chapter of "Tobah" from the Koran.

4) Think about what Allah has promised the good believers and the martyrs. Remind yourself to listen and obey that night because you will be exposed to critical situations (100%). Train and

convince yourself to do that. Allah narrated: "Obey Allah and his messenger and fall into no disputes. Lest you lose heart and your power depart and be patient and persevering for Allah is with those who are patient." (Sura VIII-46).

5) Increase your supplication to Allah with regard to aid and stability and victory in order to facilitate your matters and shield you from harm.

6) Increase your supplications to Allah and know that the best way to do so is by reciting the Koran. This is the consensus of all Islamic scholars and it's sufficient that this is the word of Allah, the Creator of the Earth and the Heavens.

7) Cleanse your heart and purify it and forget everything involving this secular life, for the time for playing is gone and it is now the time for truth. How much of our lives have we lost? Should we not use these hours that we have to perform acts of nearness and obedience to Allah?

8) Let your chest be open because it's only moments before you begin a happy life and eternal bliss with the Prophets and the veracious and martyrs and the righteous and these are the best of companions. We ask Allah of His bounties and be optimistic because the Prophet was optimistic in all his matters.

9) Establish your goal as one to become patient and to know how to behave and be steadfast and

to know that what's going to hit you would not have missed you and what has missed you would not have hit you. This is a test from Allah the Almighty to raise you up high and forgive your sins. You must acknowledge that these are only moments in which you'll be raised with gratitude from Allah, the Almighty, with rewards.

"Did you think that you would enter paradise without Allah testing those of you who struggled in his cause and remained steadfast?" (Sura III-142).

10) Also remember the sayings of Allah in which he stated: "You did indeed wish for death before you met it. Now you have seen it with your own eyes and you flinch." (Sura III-143) "How often, by Allah's will has a small force vanquished a large one?" (Sura II-249) "If Allah helps you, none can overcome you and if He forsakes you, Who is there, after that that can help you? In Allah, then, let the believers place their trust." (Sura III-160).

11) Remind yourself of the supplications and ponder their implications during the morning and the evening, etc.

12) Say your supplications and blow your breath on yourself and on your belongings (luggage, clothes, knife, ID, passport, and all your documents).

13) Inspect your arm . . . prior to your departure.

"Let one of you sharpen your blade and let him ease his sacrifice."

14) Tie your clothes around you in the same way our good forefathers had done before you. Wear tight socks that would hold on your shoes and wouldn't allow your shoes to slip off. These precautions we are expected to follow. Allah is our sufficiency, how excellent a Trustee!

15) Pray your morning prayers with a group and think of the reward while reciting your supplications and never leave your apartment without absolution because the angels will seek your forgiveness and will pray for you as long as you have ablution.

"Did you then think that we had created you in jest and that you would not be brought back to us for account?" (Sura XXIII-115).

16) Shave and wash yourself.

One of the Companions of the Prophet Muhammad said: The Prophet ordered us to read the following before going into battle, so we read it and we were safe.

The Second Phase

After this, the second stage begins:

If the taxi takes you to the airport, repeat the supplication one should recite upon riding a vehicle and upon entering a city or any other place you enter.

Smile and be at peace with yourself because Allah is with the believers and because the angels guard you even though you may not be aware. Allah is mightier than all his creations.

"Oh Allah suffice them with whatever You wish." And say "Oh Allah, we . . ." and say "Oh Allah, put a barrier in front of them and a barrier behind them and further, cover them up so that they cannot see." (Sura XXXVI-9) and say "Allah is our sufficiency, how excellent a Trustee!" remembering His word most high.

"Men say to them: 'A great army is gathering against you so fear them,' but it only increased their faith, they said: 'Allah is our sufficiency, how excellent a Trustee!'" (Sura III-173).

After you say these verses, you will notice that things will go smooth as Allah has promised His servants of his bounties that they will never be harmed as long as they follow the instructions of Allah.

"And they returned with grace and bounty from Allah; No harm ever touched them; for they followed the good pleasure of Allah and Allah is the lord of bounties unbounded." "It is only the evil one that suggests to you the fear of his. . . . Be you not afraid of them, but fear Me if you have faith." (Sura III-175).

Those are who admired the Western civilizations

and who were nourished with the love and they were scared of their weak equipment. "Be you not afraid of them, but fear Me if you have faith." (Sura III-175).

The real fear is the fear of Allah because none knows it except the believers. It is He, the One and Only, who has everything in His Hand. It is the believers who are most certain that Allah will nullify the plots of the unbelievers. "That is because Allah is He who makes feeble the plans and strategies of the unbelievers." (Sura VIII-18).

You have to know that the best invocation is to not let others notice that you are invoking, because if you say it for 1,000 times no one will be aware whether you are only silent or invoking. Even when you say "No God but Allah" (while you are smiling and reflecting upon it, then it becomes the greatest word. And it suffices that it is the statement of Unity, which you have accepted the same way as the Prophet Muhammad (peace and blessings be upon him) and the Companions, from their time until the Day of Judgment.

Don't manifest any hesitation and control yourself and be joyful with ease, because you are embarking upon a mission that Allah is pleased with. And you will be rewarded by living with the inhabitants of heaven. "Smile to hardship O youth, because you are on your way to Paradise!" In other words, any action you perform, and any invocation you repeat, Allah will be with you and the believers to protect them and grant them success, and enable them to achieve victory.

The Third Phase

When you board the plane, remember that this is a battle in the sake of Allah, which is worth the whole world and all that is in it, as the Messenger (peace and blessings be upon him) has said.

And when you sit in your seat, invoke the known supplications, and then be confident with the remembrance of Allah.: "O you who believe, if you meet an army, then stand firm and invoke Allah much so that you may prosper." (Sura VIII-45).

And when the plane takes off, remember the supplication of travels, for you are traveling to Allah, and what a beautiful travel!

This will be the hour. Then ask Allah Most High as He said in His Book: "Our Lord, pour constancy on us and make our steps firm, help us against those that reject faith." (Sura II-250) And His saying: "Our Lord, forgive us our sins, and anything we may have done that transgressed our duty. Establish our feet firmly, and help us against those that resist faith." (Sura III-147).

And remember the saying of our Prophet (peace and blessings be upon him): "O Allah, revealer of the Book, and mover of the clouds, and defeater of the party, defeat them and make us victorious over them.... Supplicate for you and your brothers, all of them, to be victorious, and do not be afraid. Ask Allah to grant you martyrdom, marching ahead, and not turning back, and be steadfast."

Let everyone be prepared to undertake his task in a way pleasing to Allah, and be courageous, as our forefathers did when they came to the battle. And in the engagement, strike the strike of the heroes, as those who don't want to go back to this life. And say, "Allah is greatest," (because it plants fear in the hearts of the unbelievers. Allah said: "Smite above their necks and smite all their finger tips." (Sura VIII-12).

And know that the Gardens of Paradise are beautified with its best ornaments, and its inhabitants are calling you. And if . . . do not let differences come between you, and listen and obey, and if you kill, then kill completely, because this is the way of the Chosen One.

On the condition that . . . there is something greater than paying attention to the enemy or attacking him, because the harm in this is much greater. For the priority of the action of the group is much more important, since this is the duty of your mission. Don't take revenge for yourself only, but make your strike and everything on the basis of doing it for the sake of Allah. As an example, Ali ibn abi Talib (may Allah be pleased with him) fought with an enemy among the infidels who spat on him, and Ali took his sword and did not strike him. When the war ended, the Companions asked him why he did not strike that person, so he said: "When he spat on me, I was afraid to strike him out of egotistic revenge for myself, so I pulled my sword out.

I wanted this to be for the sake of Allah." Then apply the way of taking captives, and do what Allah said in His Book: "It is not fitting for a Prophet that he should have prisoners of war until he has thoroughly subdued the land. You look for the temporal goods of this world, but Allah looks to the Hereafter, and Allah is Mighty, Wise." (Sura VIII-67).

Let each one of you then tap on the shoulder of his brother . . . and remind each other that this work is for the sake of Allah, and do not be afraid. And give him glad tidings, encourage each other (scratched word). And how beautiful it would be if one read some verses of the Koran, such as, "Let those fight in the cause of Allah who sell the life of this world for the Hereafter." (Sura III-74)

And: "Say not of those who are slain in the way of Allah, 'They are dead,' no, they are living." (II-154) And other similar verses that our forefathers used to mention in the battlefield, so that they bring peace to their brothers, and make tranquility and happiness enter their hearts.

Do not forget to take some booty, even if it be a
cup of water with which you drink and offer your
brothers to drink, if possible. And then when the
zero hour comes, open your chest and welcome
death in the cause of Allah, always remembering
your prayers to ease your mission before the goal
in seconds. And let your last words be, "There
is no God but Allah, and Muhammad is His
Messenger." And then comes the meeting in the
Highest Paradise with the mercy of Allah. When
you see the masses of the infidels, remember those
parties that numbered about 10,000 and how
Allah granted victory to the believers. Allah said:
"When the believers saw the confederate forces
they said, "This is what Allah and His Messenger
promised, and Allah and His Messenger told us
what was true." And it only added to their faith
and their submission." (Sura XXXIII-22).

This letter was also transmitted by CNN with the Arabic
text. I quoted this whole letter to show the terrorist's motivation. The terrorist leaders psyched up these young men to
blast themselves into eternity while they themselves hid in
caves in Afghanistan.

If being killed while fighting jihad is a direct flight to
paradise, why were these leaders hiding? Why did they not
come out to meet the American-led troops and open their
own chests to angry missiles and die joyfully?

When Afghanistan was invaded, Osama instructed his

aides to shoot him if Americans closed in on him and he could not escape (that is, if Allah failed to defend him in the end). He said he preferred to die in the hand of his companions, his closest friends, his fellow Muslim fighters, than die in the hand of infidels.

Osama is a smart man. He knew his friends would kill him gently. But if he did not die in the hand of his enemies while fighting, he would not have died by jihad. To die in the hand of fellow Muslims and personal friends is no longer a jihad. By this he would lose the privileges meant exclusively for those who die fighting.

It is not only deception but also hypocrisy and wickedness to send others to die, then hide in fortified bunkers. It has always been the case; most of the sponsors of religious terrorism live in their wealthy palaces. For example, the religious riots in Nigeria have always been sponsored by Muslims who are too rich to die now.

After reading the terrorists letter, U.S. Attorney General John Ashcroft described it as a "disturbing and shocking view of Islam, not representative of Muslims or the Islamic faith." I have due regard for Mr. Ashcroft and all those who express similar views. But the major problem with America is that we think we know Islam even more than Muslims!

On a program on CNN, Dr. Daniel Pipes, Director of Middle East Forum, a well-informed commentator on the Middle East problems who is a columnist with the *New York Post* and *Jerusalem Post*, said:

> I note that some Islamists use violence and

> some don't. But this is circumstantial. The
> person who doesn't use it (violence) today
> will use it tomorrow. They're all gunning
> for the same totalitarian goal, and which
> methods they are using at this moment I
> don't consider important at all. …I would
> say that's like making distinction between
> mainstream Nazis and fringe Nazis. They
> are all Nazis…

The terrorists want to destroy America because they are angry with America, Israel and Christianity. This issue is therefore beyond overthrowing the Taliban government in Afghanistan. Even if *Al Qaeda* is dismantled and the leaders are killed, Islamic terrorism will not end. The problem is not just *Al Qaeda*. If the Western world does not begin to see practical Islam and its god as they really are, there can be no solution. The terrorists are modeling their lives and ideology after Muhammad.

Unfortunately, the history of Islam is on their side. Out of twenty top terrorists on the FBI list, ten are named "Ahmad" or "Muhammad." In our democratic world, we will not sacrifice our freedom for anything. But is it not time we became careful about a system that has undermined our peace and freedom?

Sixteen out of the nineteen September 11 attackers came to the United States on student visas. About 600,000 are still in the country with student visas. How do we know who is capable of doing the next havoc? After all, Muhammad Attah, who led the hijackers, was said to be a normal "mainstream" gentle, quiet Muslim —until he manifested! This confirms the opinion of Daniel Pipes. Now some of them relocated to Latin America, when sentiments in the United States began to change against them.

The major responsibility of the church is evangelizing the Muslims living in America, Europe and Latin America. It is only a change in the nature of a Muslim that can make him behave well. This is true of ALL human beings. Such change is done only by the power of the Gospel of Christ.

Moreover, our governments must adopt policies that will give some restrictions to the full expression of the 7th century Islam in this century. This is a truth not many people are ready to face. We do not hate Muslims. We must love them as Jesus loves them. They have freedom to worship whatever or whoever they like. But a full expression of a religion that endangers our own lives and liberty must be curtailed. That is the stubborn truth.

There must also be sanctions on Islamic nations for their dictatorship and repression of human conscience. Saudi Arabia must be sanctioned. No churches are allowed there. About one-third of the Saudi population comprises expatriates, many of whom are Christians. For their years of stay there, they have no right to attend any church service. They must meet secretly to study the Bible and pray.

When discovered, they can be imprisoned and deported. They must not display any Christian symbol like the cross, the Bible or any Christian literature. As of this writing, there are reports of midnight raids on Christian homes, dragging some to prison for practicing Christianity. Computers containing software Bibles, books and tapes are confiscated. This is a flagrant violation of Articles 18 and 19 of the International Covenant on Civil and Political Rights of 1966.

It is criminal for the government of America to keep ignoring all these atrocities being done to Christians and continue making friends with this system in order to buy their oil. It is greed.

There is probably more oil in Alaska than in any Islamic nation. But America reserves its own oil, and does not yet realize that the control of oil by the Arab world is used as part of Jihad. Their huge investments are part of conquering the West.

An expert on Islamic history and politics and former Muslim of Pakistani descent, Patrick Sookhdeo, said:

> For a number of years, Christian communities have suffered excessive problems at the hands of Muslims. Generally, the Western nations have opted to deny the existence of such difficulties. They have oil interests, they have geopolitical interests and they are concerned with their bread-and-butter issues. Therefore, why take up issues relating to Christian minorities when there is nothing to be gained by it? We can rescue Kuwait because there is oil, but why should we want to rescue black Sudanese Christians (Indonesian Christians, Nigerian Christians and those in Saudi Arabia). It is as simple as that. ... In Britain today, where Islam con-

trols the inner cities, we have major social
exclusion and the development of Sharia.
We have had churches burned, Christians
attacked and a mission center destroyed.
The media has deliberately kept everything
off the air.[3]

Late in November 2001, three large villages, Tangkura,
Sangginova and Dewua, in Poso (Central Sulawesi) of Indonesia were leveled by Muslim jihadist warriors. Why? Because
they were almost completely Christian. Even though this was
widely reported by the press in Indonesia, the Western world
did nothing. Our press also was mysteriously silent. It didn't
concern them because it was a war against Christians.

The Saudi Arabian government has always been as dangerous and wicked as the Taliban Islamic regime of Afghanistan. The Taliban government was partly a creation of the
Wahabist Islamic persuasion of Saudi Arabia. Why then are
Saudi and Pakistan against "terrorists?" Because the same
enemies of America want to have the present Saudi government toppled.

Many Arabs all over the world who have been exposed
to freedom have always wished that Saudi citizens would rise
and overthrow the oppressive dynasty and start a democratic
society where people can be themselves.

The sight of many Afghans openly shaving their beards
and women throwing away their veils immediately after the
fall of the Taliban Islamic government shows clearly that it

3) *Washington Times*, January 16, 2002.

is just a few greedy rulers who are using Islam to oppress people and force them to behave in a particular way.

It also shows how the Saudis and other Muslims in all Islamic countries will rejoice when the various Islamic dictatorships collapse.

Meanwhile, serious propaganda continues in America to show the beauty and "peacefulness" of Islam. History is being rewritten. Jihad is being downplayed as normal peaceful struggle in life. What the American government will not allow to be taught about Christianity is being taught about Islam in some high schools in California.

Thomas More Law Center in Michigan took a school in Byron to court for an Islamic brainwashing program that seventh graders were being forced to do. Under the curriculum, all the students must adopt the speech of pious Muslims, simulate a jihad, act out the Five Pillars of Islam, greet one another as "*assalam aleikum*, fellow Muslims," wash their hands and sit on prayer rugs.

They are expected to dress like Muslims during the several weeks of this course. Students unwilling to wear Islamic clothes must sit in the back of the class mute.[4] It is a simulation that opens the minds of these kids to the influence of the spirit of Islam.

The United States of America fought with great determination the political cult called Communism. But the people of America do not understand that Islam is as dangerous and oppressive as Communism.

4) *Jerusalem Post*, July 2, 2002.

In a letter to the U.S. Senate after the September 11 attack, Frans J.L. Zegers an Indonesian, born Dutch, wrote from Holland:

> Only because Communism did not declare itself to be a religion but rather declared religion to be the opiate of the people and fought against it that the West defined it as an enemy and faced it with single-minded determination and deployment of its resources.
>
> But though Islam has openly declared its goal is world control, absolutely totalitarian in a way far worse than Communism, the West allows its infiltration, existence and free expression in its very house under the guise of freedom of religion and refuses to address the issue of absolute denial of freedom in Islamic nations of all religions and thoughts outside of Islam....
>
> How this world would have looked if Communism had openly declared that it is (and in truth it is) a religion? Then the USA and the rest of the world would, under the freedom of religion, have been forced to allow Communists and Communism to have full freedom to exist, grow, make converts and express itself.

Islam is not just a religion. It has its own economic and political agenda. Whatever makes Communism dangerous to the West makes Islam a culprit. We must resist religious savagery with the same intensity we did Communism. If we are to survive and continue enjoying our freedom, we must know and face our real enemy.

As Christians, we must realize that neither Arabs nor Muslims of any race are our enemies, whatever they may think of us. It is unchristian of us to hate them. Having experienced their hatred, the temptation is there.

Our real enemy is the spirit that inspires them against us. They are lovable people Jesus also died for. I have prayed and fasted for Muslims for about two decades. God has used me in many ways to win thousands of them to the Lord Jesus. I have personally suffered persecution at their hands. Yet I have some of them as personal friends.

As Christians we have the mandate from our Lord to show Muslims the love of Christ. We cannot fight them as a people. We must know who our real enemy is. We don't attack people; we attack beliefs and the gods of destructive beliefs. Beliefs are more dangerous than people. It is the beliefs that motivate people to act. Proverbs 23:7 says, *"As he (a man) thinketh in his heart, so is he."*

America says she is fighting terrorism. But who is a terrorist? If we do not locate our enemy we cannot dislocate him. We have heard world leaders say that the words and deeds of the terrorists are not representative of Muslims or the Islamic faith.

We must be careful to differentiate between opinions and historical facts, current experiences, and the Qur'an.

Sometimes the ignorance or hypocrisy of our political leaders is more terrifying than the terror attacks of Muslims. Like some other leaders, Mr. Tony Blair has said consistently that Islam is synonymous with "peace, tolerance and a force for good." But what are the facts... in history... in the revered books of Islam, the Qur'an... and the *Hadith*?

Maybe we are so engulfed with the present that we forgot history. When Muhammad died, his first four successors (Caliphs) were all murdered by other Muslims. Between 1948 (when Israel became a nation) and 1973, there were 80 revolutions in the Arab world, 30 of them were successful.

Twenty-two heads of state were murdered during this period. In the eight-year war between two Islamic nations, Iran and Iraq, there were one million deaths, more deaths than in World War I. Has Islam ever brought peace among Muslims? But we hear that Islam is synonymous with "peace, tolerance and a force for good." Now, let us listen to Allah, the inspirer of Islam:

> ...I will cast terror into the hearts of those
> who have disbelieved, so strike them over
> the necks, and smite over all their fingers
> and toes.[5]

Who then is the terrorist we are looking for? Any serious Muslim who is devoted to Allah and wants to obey him completely is potentially dangerous to a non-Muslim neighbor. In the verse above, Allah says he is the one that inspires the terror. Again Allah says:

5) Sura 8:12 (Hilali and Khan).

...the disbelievers (all non-Muslims) are
ever unto you open enemies.[6]

O you who believe (Muslims)! Fight those
of the disbelievers who are close to you, and
let them find harshness in you, and know
that Allah is with those who are Al-Mut-
taqun (the pious).[7]

This is Allah talking! Does that mean the pious Muslim
is most dangerous to his non-Muslim neighbors?

FIGHTING FUNDAMENTALISM?

Fundamentalism is not evil. What is evil is being a fundamentalist in a wrong religion or ideology. The *Concise
Oxford Dictionary* defines fundamentalism as "the strict
maintenance of the ancient and fundamental doctrines of
any religion or ideology."

The Islamic fundamentalist believes Allah is speaking
in the Qur'an and he must obey all that Allah says. He
believes in all the sayings of Muhammad and wants to live
like Muhammad.

A Christian fundamentalist believes he must live his
life strictly as Jesus taught in the Bible, hating sin in all its
expressions and preaching the Gospel of Christ the way
Christ preached it.

What is the fruit of each of these forms of fundamentalism? One leads to fear, terror and oppression. The other

6) Sura 4:10 (Hilali and Khan).
7) Sura 9:123 (Hilali and Khan) et al.

leads to love, joy, peace and freedom in the society. When our lawmakers say they are attacking fundamentalism, they must define their terms.

Former Muslim and present Anglican priest, Patrick Sookhdeo, said:

> I think we have a greater problem with Islam
> than we realize. Much as I understand why
> politicians in the U.S. and U.K. have made
> the kinds of affirmatory statements they
> have made (about Islam), I think time will
> show they have made a mistake. In dealing
> with Islam, you have to tell the truth. And
> you have to meet it head on. It understands
> power and only power. And so you have to
> know how to exercise power.[8]

Islam has always proved by its teachings and practices that it is out to exterminate non-Muslims. On October 2, 1996, the Nigerian Television Authority (NTA) aired a news story of a Qur'anic recitation competition organized by a national association of Muslims in Nigeria. First prize was two swords, some cash awards and a wall clock. The winners were told they would represent Nigeria at an international competition in Saudi Arabia.

Why were two swords a reward for knowing the Qur'an? The flag of Saudi Arabia has two swords on it! What do swords represent?

While some of our lawmakers promote Islam, they are

8) *Washington Times*, January 16, 2002.

making efforts to stifle evangelization by Christians. Some even classify evangelistic Christian literature for homosexuals and Muslims as "hate literature." But they have not classified the Qur'an with all its incitements.

WARS IN THE BIBLE

CHAPTER FOUR

READING THROUGH the Old Testament of the Bible, we find wars. One may ask: why were there wars if the God of the Bible is a God of peace?

He is indeed a God of love and peace; but He also has a hatred for SIN because He is holy. His holiness demands judgment; yet he still bears long with man's wickedness.

He helped the Israelites defeat the enemies that came against them, not just because He loves Israel (though He does[1]) but because He hates the sin of these other nations.

The grace the Israelites enjoyed in the Old Testament was because their forebears, Abraham, Isaac and Jacob, believed God and it was "counted unto [them] for righteousness."[2]

1) The Qur'an proves this truth in Sura 2:40, 47, 122.
2) See Romans 4:3 and Hebrews 11.

While many people in other parts of the world gave them-selves to idols, built images, and called them the God that made the heaven and the earth, the ancestors of the Israelites knew and followed the true God wholeheartedly. God says He punishes the children for the sin of the fathers to:

> ...the third and fourth generation of them
> that hate me; and shewing MERCY unto
> thousands of them that love me, and keep
> my commandments.[3]

Some of the nations the Israelites fought against were destroyed because, instead of accepting the God of Israel, they tempted Israel to worship idols (Numbers 25:1-10).

But even then, God did not instruct His people to kill anybody they met on the way to Canaan. These nations committed many unprintable sins in Canaan, influencing the Israelites to turn from the true God to idolatry, astrology, human sacrifices, and especially burning their own children alive to the idol Molech (Deuteronomy 12:30-31).

Because of His holiness, God also had to destroy Israel because they were lured into the sins of these Moabites and other idolaters. God told Israel that if they indulged in the wickedness of these Canaanites, He would punish them.

In fact, Israel has suffered more for idolatry than any nation in the world. God has dealt with them more than their enemies. God chose to use them to reveal the true God to the world. But this privilege carried a great responsibility. There was a level of sin that certain nations got away with

3) Exodus 20:5-6.

without serious punishment from the LORD. But not so with Israel. Through the Prophet Amos, God told Israel:

> …You only have I known of all the families of the earth: therefore I will punish you for all your iniquities.[4]

The first war the Israelites fought was a direct assault from the Amalekites. There was a shorter way from Egypt to Canaan, but the Amalekites were there. So God took them through a hazardous wilderness to avoid any confrontation (and to take the sinful practices of Egypt out of them). But as they were resting at Rephidim, the Amalekites suddenly struck— unprovoked, determined to destroy Israel.

Moses sought the face of the Lord and then sent Joshua and some chosen men to the battlefield. With the help of God, the Amalekites were defeated. (See Exodus 17:8-13.)

> And the LORD said unto Moses, Write this for a memorial in a book, and rehearse it in the ears of Joshua: for I will utterly put out the remembrance of Amalek from under heaven.[5]

It was for this that God later commanded King Saul to destroy the Amalekites.[6] Many other nations which heard the fame of Israel's encounter in Egypt decided to attack them whenever they heard of them coming through their land:

> Let us pass, I pray thee, through thy country: we will not pass through the fields or

4) Amos 3:1-2.
5) Exodus 17:14.
6) See 1 Samuel 15:1-3.

> through the vineyards, neither will we drink
> of the water of the wells: we will go by the
> king's high way, we will not turn to the
> right hand nor to the left, until we have
> passed thy borders.[7]

So Moses made an oath and pleaded with the King of
Edom. But the king refused, and they had to turn back:

> And when king Arad the Canaanite, which
> dwelt in the south, heard tell that Israel
> came by the way of the spies; then he fought
> against Israel, and took some of them pris-
> oners. And Israel vowed a vow unto the
> LORD, and said, If thou wilt indeed deliver
> this people into my hand, then I will utterly
> destroy their cities. And the LORD har-
> kened to the voice of Israel, and delivered up
> the Canaanites; and they utterly destroyed
> them and their cities....[8]

That was the second war Israel fought after they left
Egypt. Again, later, with the Amorites:

> And Israel sent messengers unto Sihon king
> of the Amorites, saying, Let me pass through
> thy land: we will not turn into the fields,
> or into the vineyards; we will not drink of
> the waters of the well: but we will go along
> by the king's high way, until we be past
> thy borders. And Sihon would not suffer

7) Numbers 20:17.
8) Numbers 21:1-3.

> Israel to pass through his border: but Sihon gathered all his people together, and went out against Israel into the wilderness: and he came to Jahaz, and fought against Israel. And Israel smote him with the edge of the sword, and possessed his land....[9]
>
> And it came to pass ... all the kings which were on this side Jordan ... gathered themselves together, to fight with Joshua and with Israel, with one accord.[10]

As did the western kings, so did the northern kings, but they were all defeated (Joshua 11). In the Old Testament, whenever Israel sinned and went to battle, they lost and died (Joshua 7). After the death of Joshua:

> ... the children of Israel did evil in the sight of the LORD, and served Baalim ... and provoked the LORD to anger. And they forsook the LORD, and served Baal and Ashtaroth. And the anger of the LORD was hot against Israel, and he delivered them into the hands of spoilers that spoiled them, and he sold them into the hands of their enemies round about, so that they could not any longer stand before their enemies. Whithersoever they went out, the hand of the LORD was against them for evil, as the LORD had said, and as the LORD had

9) Numbers 21:21-24.
10) Joshua 9:1-2.

sworn unto them: and they were greatly
distressed.[11]

Even though God was with Israel, He is so holy He will
NOT tolerate sin forever. Whenever rebellion filled the camp
of Israel, thousands of souls had to die for it.

When they made a molten calf to represent the God
that brought them out of Egypt, the LORD's anger burned
against them and He decided to wipe them off the earth! He
would have done so but for the intercession of Moses:

> And I fell down before the LORD, as at
> the first, forty days and forty nights: I did
> neither eat bread, not drink water, because
> of all your sins which ye sinned, in doing
> wickedly in the sight of the LORD, to pro-
> voke him to anger.[12]

Even though God did not destroy the whole of Israel
that day, about 3,000 people died. (Exodus 32:28)

People who think they can worship anything in the name
of the culture of their forefathers, or modern man who leaves
the Creator and worships the creation (nature), should know
that the fearful judgment of God is hanging upon them, no
matter how long it may take:

> Because sentence against an evil work is
> not executed speedily, therefore the heart
> of the sons of men is fully set in them to
> do evil.[13]

11) Judges 2:11-15.
12) Deuteronomy 9:18.
13) Ecclesiastes 8:11.

> Though hand join in hand, the wicked (sinner) shall not be unpunished: but the seed of the righteous shall be delivered.[14]

God told the children of Israel how He was going to destroy the nations beyond the Jordan to the Promised Land. But Moses pronounced emphatically:

> Not for thy righteousness, or for the uprightness of thine heart, dost thou go to possess their land: but for the wickedness of these nations the LORD thy God doth drive them out from before thee, and that he may perform the word which the LORD sware unto thy fathers, Abraham, Isaac and Jacob.[15]

Jesus said, "My kingdom is not of this world."[16] So there were no wars in the New Testament between Christians and the heathen. There was no land to fight over. The Christians subjected themselves to the cruelty of the rulers of their days. In fact, one reason why the Jews rejected Jesus was because He did not prove to be the leader that would lead them to overthrow their European oppressors (the Romans).

Paul says: "If God be for us, who can be against us?"[17] However, Allah asks Muslims to attack the Jews.[18] He sounds like the kings of the Amorites, the King of Jericho, Adonizedek, and all those who rose against the Jews.

14) Proverbs 11:21.
15) Deuteronomy 9:5.
16) John 18:36.
17) Romans 8:31.
18) Sura 9:29 (Hilali and Khan).

"Destroy the Jews" has always been the cry of the heathen from Old Testament days until today. That was the same cry of Haman in Esther 3:8-9; it was the cry of Adolf Hitler, who slaughtered more than six million Jews.

But the seed of Abraham shall never perish from the earth, no matter how fierce the animosity of the enemies of their God. The question is still: Who is this Allah that is so incensed against God's people?

Jews have suffered the most in the world as a nation, starting with their 430 years of slavery in Egypt. Yet it pleased the LORD that the Saviour of the world should come through them, "for salvation is of the Jews" (John 4:22).

Yes, the true God is a God of peace, but there is no peace without obedience to His laws. His laws are designed to promote a peaceful society. Violation of those laws brings much trouble and hurt. Thus, those who are set on rebelling against those laws must be dealt with, and war is often the instrument God uses to punish or eliminate the rebels.

Muslims claim their laws also bring peace, but not a peace with love, joy and freedom. Their laws promote violence, revenge, oppression and hatred, —war for subjugation, not for correction in righteousness.

CHRISTIAN WARFARE

CHAPTER FIVE

CHRISTIANITY IS WARFARE. But Christ proclaimed victory at His resurrection. Paul described the strategy, that our weapons are spiritual, not by worldly means of the flesh.[1]

The famous Arabic poet, Ahmad Shawgi, embarrassed the Muslim world when he wrote how Jesus fought and won through a different means than Muslims. He says the Cross was wood, not iron of a sharp side. Speaking in another poem, written as a tribute to Christ on a Christmas day, he says:

> Essa, your way, mercy and love, of inno-
> cence among men, and peace as a dove. You
> were not the one to shed blood, nor one that
> neglected the weak, nor the orphan.[2]

1) See 2 Corinthians 10:4.
2) Translated by F. Barsoum

Christians serve the God of the Bible. Our real enemy is Satan, and he was defeated by the events of the Cross and the Resurrection. All others who hate us, humans and demons, are just his servants and agents, and we know how best to deal with them. According to the gospel of Jesus Christ:

> The servant of the Lord must not strive;
> but gentle to all men, apt to teach, patient,
> in meekness instructing those that oppose
> themselves; if God peradventure will give
> them repentance to the acknowledging of
> the truth; And that they may recover them-
> selves out of the snare of the devil, who are
> taken captive by him at his will.[3]

Because we have such teachings we do not fight physically. Christians have "the mind of Christ" (1 Corinthians 2:16). The Qur'an acknowledges Christians as loving everybody, including their Muslim enemies. (Sura 5:82-85).

Our God is a God of love. According to the Scriptures, *"the love of God is* (supernaturally*) shed abroad in our hearts by the Holy Ghost"* at the time of our conversion (Romans 5:5b). This kind of love cannot be faked; nor can anyone have it except he is born of and by the Spirit. Muslims may fake many things in Christianity, but they can't fake our love. Jesus told some religious people:

> …If God were your Father, ye would LOVE
> me: for I proceeded forth and came from God:
> neither came I of myself, but he sent me.

---

3) 2 Timothy 2:24-26.

Ye are of your father the devil, and the lusts
of your father ye will do. He was a murderer
from the beginning, and abode not in the
truth, because there is no truth in him.
When he speaketh a lie, he speaketh of his
own: for he is a liar, and the father of it.[4]

The Bible talks of Christians fighting and warring. But it makes it clear that:

We wrestle not against flesh and blood
(physical human beings), but against princi-
palities, against powers, against the rulers of
the darkness of this world, against spiritual
wickedness in high places.[5]

Therefore:

"...the weapons of our warfare are not carnal
(physical arm, swords, guns, knives, matches
and petrol), but MIGHTY through God to
the pulling down of strong holds.[6]

We have never been moved by the provocative Islamic pamphlets and tapes of Muslim writers, or by sermons of Islamic preachers in many parts of the world. We do not have to fight physically to defend the truth. That is God's job.

We win with spiritual weapons, not physical weapons. The Apostle Paul enumerated the six weapons of the Christian warfare. Not one is physical, they are all spiritual:[7]

4) John 8:42, 44.
5) Ephesians 6:12.
6) 2 Corinthians 10:4.
7) Ephesians 6:10-18.

For though we walk in the flesh, we do not war after the flesh: (For the weapons of our warfare are not carnal (physical), but mighty through God to the pulling down of strong holds;) Casting down imaginations, and every high thing that exalteth itself against the knowledge of God, and bringing into captivity every thought to the obedience of Christ."[8]

Jesus rebuked Peter for using a physical sword to defend Him, then restored the ear that was cut off, teaching Peter that not fighting physically did not mean He was weak, but that He had an eternal plan. Long before He died, Jesus said:

"Therefore doth my Father love me, because I lay down my life, that I might take it again. No man taketh it from me, but I lay it down of myself. I have power to lay it down, and I have power to take it again. This commandment have I received from my Father."[9]

WHAT ABOUT THE CRUSADES?

The Crusades took place from 1096 until the early 13th Century to regain Jerusalem from Arab and Turkish Muslims. These wars are generally regarded as wars between Christians and Muslims and have often been used by Muslim writers as proof of the "violence" of Christianity.

8) 2 Corinthians 10:3-5.
9) John 10:17-18.

But the fact that these wars were between Europe and the Islamic and Turkish rulers does not make them religious. The assumption is that the "Christian" Europe was warring against the Muslims.

The Crusades were political wars engineered by kings and emperors and the apostate papacy, which wanted to annex Jerusalem, but felt the Turks had been a little faster. Apart from the terrible loss of lives, including children, Peter the Hermit, Godfrey of Bouillion, Gottschalk and all their Crusaders, including the Catholic Pope Urban II, who engineered the whole thing, failed because the wars were not God's.

Even though the Crusaders went out with the sign of the cross, they were not Christians. Unfortunately, Muslims do not know the difference between Biblical Christianity and the motivation of those involved in the barbaric Crusades. The Crusaders did not know that Jesus had said:

> "…Jerusalem shall be trodden down of the
> Gentiles until the times of the Gentiles be
> fulfilled (run their course)."[10]

Jesus was explaining to His disciples what would happen to the Holy Land because it had rejected His Lordship. He said it was a punishment *that all things which are written may be fulfilled* (Luke 21:22). He warned the disciples to flee when things began to happen. Daniel and Jesus prophesied *"the abomination of desolation."*[11]

Jesus Christ came through the Jewish race and to them

10) Luke 21:24.
11) See Luke 21:20-24 and Daniel 11:31 for a better understanding.

first. But they rejected Him, saying, *"We have no king but Caesar."* Several "Caesars" all over the world have ruled and oppressed them since then. They said, *"We do not want this man (Jesus) to be King over us."* They handed Him over to the Europeans (Romans) to be killed, and then swore:

His blood be on us and on our children."[12]

This was literally fulfilled on them. About twenty years after the death of Christ (50 A.D), they had some clashes with the Roman government and 30,000 of them perished.

Twelve years after, Ben Kuchtba led them in a revolt against the oppressive reign of Governor Gessius Florus, and Emperor Nero had to send Vespasian to quell the riot. At the end of the operation, 40,000 Jews were slaughtered.

Four years later, (i.e. 70 A.D), General Titus, who had followed his father, Vespasian, on the previous operation, went back to Jerusalem with 100,000 men. In August, after four months of siege, Jerusalem was captured. According to Josephus Flavius, an authority on Jewish history, over one million Jews were killed during this invasion.

The Temple that the Jews had cherished more than the Son of God was completely leveled, exactly the way Jesus said (Matthew 24:1-2). Many of them were dispersed all over the world.

But their suffering did not end there. In 130 A.D., Hadrian, the emperor of Rome, erected the statue of Jupiter on the Temple area. This was a great abomination and thus aroused the wrath of the Jews who remained in Jerusalem.

12) Matthew 27:25.

It led to an insurrection that resulted in another massacre of the people in 135 A.D. The dispersal continued.

Another emperor, Julian, who came to power in 361 A.D. knew of this prophecy of Jesus, how the Temple would be completely destroyed and not be rebuilt until the fullness of time. In an attempt to falsify this prophecy, Julian (known in history as Julian the Apostate) decided to rebuild the Temple. But he failed:

> His (Julian's) attempt to rebuild the temple at Jerusalem was intended to falsify the prophecies of Christianity no less than to please the Jews; the balls of flame which brought the work to a standstill were accepted as evidence of the interposition of heaven.[13]

Barely six years after the death of Muhammad in 638 A.D., Muhammad's followers also came with swords and conquered and occupied Jerusalem. When Jerusalem finally fell, these invaders had slaughtered over 90,000 "Christians."

Today, you find the Mosque of Omar at a site very near that former majestic and glorious Solomon's Temple, where, instead of the cloud of the glory of Jehovah, we hear regular chants of *la illaha* to a certain Allah. That Mosque took half a century to complete.

Jews, who yearn for God, still go to a place near the Temple site to wail for their sins beside the Wailing Wall. Muslims, not satisfied with encroaching on the Temple Mount, con-

---

13) *New Standard Encyclopedia*, Vol. XVI, pg. 509.

stantly heave stones from inside the Mosque at the praying Israelis around the Wailing Wall.

On October 8, 1990, the provocation reached a stage and the Israeli police opened fire on the Muslims, killing 21. This sparked condemnation from the international community.

Another imposing mosque, El-Aksa Mosque, was erected on Abraham's grave at Hebron.

The Christian's most holy place on earth, the top of Mount Calvary, where the Son of God shed His holy blood, became a Muslim cemetery! Also, the Bible says the anti-Christ will set himself up to be worshipped in the temple of God. (2 Thessalonians 2:3-4).

This is part of the abomination of desolation standing where it does not belong, as Jesus prophesied in Mark 13:14. But the Bible is clear that "the times of the Gentiles" will surely expire in all these places, and very soon.

Part of this has been fulfilled and more is being fulfilled before our very eyes. As for the final dissolution of these Gentiles in this ancient holy city, the Spirit of the Lord will raise a standard against the enemies.

For Christians, our weapons of warfare are greater than any atomic bomb the world can ever dream of inventing. The "Crusades" of today mean rescuing souls from the hand of the devil, for *"knowing therefore the terror of the Lord, <u>we persuade</u> men"* to turn away from sin and false religions and receive the gift of salvation offered through Christ Jesus (2 Corinthians 5:11).

When King David, in his pietistic zeal, nursed the idea of building that great temple for the Lord, God said:

> "Thou shalt not build an house for my name, because thou hast been a man of war, and hast shed blood."[14]

Many early mosques built by Muhammad and his successors and even the mosque of Omar standing at the site of that Temple were built with hands of blood. Allah delights in that and promises them rewards in heaven.

We can be sure that the God of the Bible is different from the god of Islam. Muslim scholars may advance arrogant arguments to defend their religion, but they can't escape the facts of their history. Facts are invincible; no intellectual arguments can demolish them.

ISLAMIC WEAPONS AGAINST SATAN

Muslims also see Satan as an enemy who should be fought. But with what weapons do they fight him? Allah recommends stones and pebbles. That is why every Muslim pilgrim who performs the *hajj* to Mecca must throw seven pebbles at a pillar regarded as The Great Satan!

That must be one of the biggest amusements Satan has every year —people trying to throw pebbles at a spirit. The speaker in the Qur'an should know better than that.

The Word of God makes it clear that for Christians the warfare is not against a being of flesh and blood or a pil-

14) 1 Chronicles 28:2-3.

lar that can be stoned.[15] Therefore it does not recommend physical weapons to fight the devil and his hosts.[16]

One is surprised that while Allah recommends pebbles to fight Satan, he commands that Christians, Jews and all non-Muslims be fought against and killed, and that converts from Islam be slain (Sura 4:89).

This is significant, and is one of the reasons we must research the identity of the Allah of Islam.

15) 2 Corinthians 10:4.
16) Ephesians 6:10-18.

THE SONSHIP OF JESUS

CHAPTER SIX

Who hath ascended up into heaven, or descended? who hath gathered the wind in his fists? who hath bound the waters in a garment? who hath established all the ends of the earth? what is his NAME, and what is HIS SON'S name, if thou canst tell?[1]

For we have not followed cunningly devised fables, when we made known to you the power and coming of our Lord Jesus Christ, but were eyewitnesses of his majesty.

For he received from God the Father honour and glory, when there came such a voice to him from the excellent glory, This is my

1) Proverbs 30:4.

beloved Son, in whom I am well pleased.

And this voice which came from heaven we heard, when we were with him in the holy mount.

We have also a more sure word of prophecy; whereunto ye do well that ye take heed, as unto a light that shineth in a dark place, until the day dawn, and the day star arise in your hearts..."[2]

THE RELATIONSHIP of Jesus Christ with God has always been the major offense to Muslims. Is Jesus the Son of God? Can God have a Son? The Bible says yes. Allah says no.

Because Christians insist that Jesus is the Son of the living God, the Qur'an says, "...*Allah's curse be on them...!*"[3]

It is impossible for a Muslim to believe all the words of the Qur'an and still believe that Jesus is the Son of God. You may ask: Did Muhammad personally develop a hatred for this fundamental truth of the Christian faith or did Allah inspire him?

Some people suggest that Muhammad had good intentions initially, but fell into the hand of a malicious *jinni* who deceived him and stood him against the Sonship and deity of Jesus Christ.

For example, the Allah of the pre-Islamic Mecca was

2) 2 Peter 1:16-19.
3 Sura 9:30 (Hilali and Khan).

said to have engendered sons and daughters. Muhammad might have felt this was improper for a Creator. Maybe that is why we hear:

> ...the primal origin of the heavens and the
> earth: How can He have a son when he
> hath no consort (wife)?[4]

This Meccan paganistic teaching is probably the idea Muhammad was against. But when he heard that the God of the Christians had a Son called Jesus, he dismissed the idea as heresy, along with the Meccans idea of the "fatherhood" of God.

Another confusion Muhammad faced was the doctrine of the Maryamiyya cults, prevalent from the 5th to the 7th century. These pagan sects believed the creator had a wife called Venus or Al Zahrah, whom they regarded as "the queen of heaven," and that they had a son by procreation.

When these people tried to become accepted as Christians, they imported the doctrine into their religion, regarding Mary as the Venus or Al-Zahrah the "queen of heaven," and Jesus as the son. They exalted and worshipped Mary as a goddess, hence they were called the Mariamists.

Genuine Christians knew this was a dangerous doctrine, and fought the heresy and broke fellowship with the adherents. By the end of the 7th century, the sects no longer existed.

It was during this period when Islam emerged. Maybe that is why many Muslims say Sura 5:116 teaches that the Christian Trinity consists of God the Father, Mary, and

4) Sura 6:101 (Yusuf Ali).

Jesus. Either Muhammad took the Mariamist doctrine as the Christian doctrine of the Trinity or he was ignorant of what Christians believe about the Holy Trinity and particularly, the Sonship of Jesus.

Others suggest that Catholicism's veneration of Mary might have compounded Muhammad's confusion. Nestorian and Arian heresies were also full-blown among Christians at that time, further adding to Muhammad's confusion.

But we must not draw a conclusion yet. The evidence that Muhammad's repudiation of the Sonship of Jesus was because of the Meccan and Mariamist doctrines is very slender, being only a suggestion drawn from some historical records.

From the Qur'an, however, it is evident that apart from the idolaters of Mecca, Muhammad considered Bible Christianity a form of heathenism. Worshipping Jesus as the Son of God was seen as idolatry. The same thing is happening today. The very idea of the Incarnation was unimaginable to Muhammad, and still is to Muslims today.

The second problem is the issue of inspiration. If Muhammad insisted that Allah was speaking through him, then we must take the matter seriously. If he said he was inspired by Allah to go against the Christian belief in the deity of Jesus, we should approach the issue from that perspective.

If Allah is indeed "All-wise, All-knowing" as is repeated everywhere in the Qur'an, he should know that the Christian doctrine of the Trinity does not include Mary, as is alleged in the Qur'an.

In the Qur'an, Allah's problem was not so much the

Trinity as it was the Sonship of Jesus. Sura 2:116 basically states: Allah has a Son? NEVER!

Sura 112, called *Al-Ikhlas,* is the key sura for all Muslims. It is repeated in their prayers everyday.

> "Say: He is Allah alone: Allah the eternal.
> He begetteth not, and he is not begotten.
> And there is none like unto him."[5]

The Sonship of Jesus is denied in several other places in the Qur'an. For example:

> "The Messiah, Jesus son of Mary, was only a
> messenger of Allah... Allah is only one Allah.
> Far is it removed from His Transcendent
> Majesty that He should have a son..."[6]

Putting Jesus on the pedestal of Sonship to God is the unforgivable sin Muslims called *shirk.* It irks them; it bites them; it nauseates them. They can't imagine it.

Because certain things about God cannot be imagined they are called "wonderful." God ceases to be God if His nature and capabilities can be logically reasoned out by the human mind. Allah is quoted in the Qur'an as saying:

> "…the Christians say: the Messiah is the son
> of Allah… Allah's Curse be on them, how
> they are deluded away from the truth!"[7]

Of course, no curse of Allah can affect a true, born-again Christian (maybe that is why Muslims use physical weapons

5) Sura 112 (Yusuf Ali).
6) Sura 4:171 (Pickthall).
7) Sura 9:30 (Hilali and Khan).

against us). We do not regret that Jesus is not the Son of Allah. It is hard to imagine the Muslim god begetting "the Prince of Peace," or a "meek and lowly" Christ.

Is there any logic in the claim of the deity of Jesus? The Bible says, *"God is a Spirit"* (John 4:24). The Qur'an says Jesus is the Spirit of God that came into Mary (Sura 21:91).

If God is a Spirit and Jesus is the Spirit of God (and we agree that the spirit and the body are distinct, yet one), then we do not need any complex logic to conclude that Jesus is one with God. We should also remember that another name of Jesus (given to Him 700 years before He was born physically) is *Immanuel,* meaning "God with us."

Jesus did not become what He is because He was born of Mary. He had been what He is before the foundation of the world. He only incarnated, that is, took on the flesh of man to save man. He emanated from God, He said:

> Sacrifice and offering thou wouldest not,
> but a body hast thou prepared me...[8]

He only came down to enter that body of Mary. Again, the Bible says Jesus is the Word of God:

> ...the Word was with God, and the Word
> was God... The Word was made flesh, and
> dwelt among us, (and we beheld his glory,
> the glory as of the only begotten of the
> Father,) full of grace and truth.[9]

In Sura 3:45, we read:

8) Hebrews 10:5.
9) John 1:1,14

> …the angels said: O Mary! Lo! Allah
> giveth thee glad tidings of a word from
> him, *whose* name is the Messiah, Jesus, son
> of Mary…[10]

Because many Muslim commentators reject anything that may suggest the deity of Jesus, they contend that the "Word" is just the creative command (fiat) of God "be." But earlier Muslim scholars in the class of Al Shaikh Muhyl Al Din Al Arabi knew better.

Al Arabi points out that the Arabic word translated "whose" in that verse is *ismihi*. It is a masculine personal pronoun. That is why the English translation has rightly used the personal relative pronoun "whose." This shows that the Word being spoken about is not just a grammatical unit, or even a power, but a person.[11]

Celebrated Arabic scholar Al'Arasi wrote: "The Word is God in theophany… and it is the one divine person."

If the Word is a person, and the Word is God, and the Word became flesh, then God became flesh. Thus, it was not that Jesus, a mere man, made himself to be God, or Christians made him so, but that God made Himself to be in Jesus, and calls him His Son, His Christ. The Qur'an says:

> "…the primal origin of the heavens and
> the earth: How can He have a son when
> He hath no consort?"[12]

10) Sura 3:45 (Pickthall).
11) Yusuf Ali's translation says "his" instead of "whose," showing this "Word" is a person.
12) Sura 6:101 (Yusuf Ali).

Notice here that this is a person other than "the Lord" speaking contrary to the claim of Muslims that all the words in the Qur'an are words being spoken by "the Lord").

But in *Hadith* Kudsi, the Lord is quoted as saying, "The rich are my agents and the poor are members of my family (my sons)." (This also disproves the Muslim claim that the *Hadith* contains only the words and deeds of Muhammad, while the Qur'an contains the words of Allah).

The writer of the Qur'an says, "when He did not have a consort (wife)." But in that *Hadith*, Allah talks of "my family." As Christians, we do not take Allah having a family to mean that he is a husband with a wife, children, inlaws, etc. We understand that *Hadith* statement to be metaphoric.

But if Muslims have such a statement in one of their sacred books, why do they object so strongly to the Christian God having a Son? Why do they have to imagine the Sonship of Jesus as of biological relationship?

God is the Father of Jesus Christ, not in a physical sense, not even in the sense of the *Hadith* quoted above, but in a very unique way that transcends limited human language and reasoning. And it is because He is the Son of God that He is God in nature. God declares Jesus His Son.

It is pride and arrogance for man to insist that he must understand everything before accepting its reality. When we receive the Christian truth by simple faith is when we begin to have a revelation of that truth in our spirit. Like the philosopher Anselm, I say: credo *ut intelligam (I believe so that I may understand.)*

Jesus told those who doubted His deity, *"If any man will do his will, he shall know of the doctrine..."* (John 7:17).

This is to say that the Deity of Jesus as the Son of God is not necessarily a simple logically provable doctrine, and it doesn't have to be. We believe it because God says so, and that settles it. Yet on the other hand, this does not mean there is no sense in the doctrine, just as we have pointed out.

With mordant invective, many Muslims tell us, "Look, you don't reason; an ordinary kindergarten pupil knows the elementary arithmetic of 1+1+1= 3 and not 1."

Yes, we agree that 1+1+1=3; but that is only in elementary arithmetic. In advanced mathematics, physics and logic, when dealing with infinity, 1+1+1 CAN equal 1! If many Muslims are really patient to reason, they won't take the doctrine of Trinity as offensive to logic. Former Nigerian Muslim Head of State Ibrahim Babangida has written:

> The confirmation and concession by the Muslims that Jesus Christ was indeed of virgin birth leaves the door open for many possibilities. Two of these possibilities are, in fact, the divinity of Jesus Christ and his divine Sonship. Philosophy agrees that there can be many in one and one manifesting many particulars just as mathematics allows that a set can have classes and subsets. The human body is a perfect example of many in one and one in many both in the philosophical and mathematical senses.

The Trinitarian doctrine is simply the belief
that God is made up absolutely of three
parts and Jesus Christ is one of them. There
is nothing to draw unnecessary offence or
blood in such a belief especially as we all
have the opportunity to know the correct
thing on the judgment day...."[13]

While this statement from Babangida is a welcome appeal
to reason and tolerance, the Bible teaches us that the question of the Person, Deity, and Work of Jesus Christ must
be settled in the heart and life of each individual while he is
still on earth. Will it be wise for us to wait until the Day of
Judgment when our discovery cannot help us? If one held
on to a wrong thing on earth, of what profit will such a
discovery be after death, if not eternal regret?

God has given us the intellect with which to reason.
When people ignore reason they get emotional if their faith
is critically examined. Yet God does not want us to have just
an intellectual agreement with His Word. Our knowledge in
the mind must lead us to a saving faith by the heart, which
then must lead us to a changed life.

Homer Duncan said thousands of people miss Heaven
by only a few inches. "By this I mean the distance between
the head and the heart"[14]

Some don't even care about logic. As long as their relatives

13) Babangida, I.B. "Man has Failed Islam and Christianity," Seminar Paper,
The Guardian, August 14, 1992, Lagos. p. 31.
14) Duncan, Homer. *Only a Few Inches*, MC International Publications,
2451-34th Street, Lubbock, TX 79411.

are in a religion, they cannot imagine leaving it because of persecution. This book is not for such people. It is for those who are ready to think if they are exposed to the facts.

God has created man in His own image, according to the Bible (Genesis 1:26-27). As a Trinity, He made man also a kind of trinity, spirit, soul and body, distinct yet one. This is wonderful. If the nature of man is a mystery, how much more the nature of God?

> And without controversy great is the mystery of godliness (i.e. the divine nature or the Arabic "uqnum"): God was manifest in the flesh, justified in the Spirit, seen of angels, preached unto the Gentiles, believed on in the world, and received up into glory.[15]

That is the summary of the New Testament Bible. It was God that sent angel Gabriel to announce to Mary:

> "The Holy Ghost shall come upon you, and the power of the Highest will overshadow you; therefore, also, that holy thing which shall be born of thee shall be called the Son of God."[16]

Six hundred and forty years later, Muhammad said an Angel Gabriel came to him with a message from Allah that Jesus was not really what the Bible says He is, and that He was just a fine prophet. The question we must answer with all sincerity is: Which (and whose) Gabriel came to him?

15) 1 Timothy 3:16.
16) Luke 1:35.

Before Muhammad came with his message, however, the Apostle Paul had already warned:

> "But though (even if) we or an angel from heaven, preach any other gospel unto you than that which we have preached unto you, let him be accursed."[17]

The reason is that only an angel of the devil can say a thing contrary to what God has already said.

God's own voice from heaven, in the presence of many witnesses, declared, *"Thou art my beloved Son; in thee I am well pleased"* (Luke 3:22).

Yes, God declared Jesus to be His Son. But Allah and his Muhammad say He cannot be. Some modern Muslims claim that the aspects of the Scriptures that present Jesus as the Son of God are adulterated Scriptures. The Bible says, *"Let God be true, but every man a liar"* (Romans 3:4).

But a Muslim who truly believes in the Qur'an cannot believe that God is so helpless that He allowed His Word to be corrupted. According to the Qur'a, corruption of the Word of God is utterly impossible.[18]

Muslim critics, commenting on the many different Bible translations today, pretend they don't know that there are about 50 different translations of their own Qur'an. At least six translations of the Qur'an honored by a majority of Muslims. Each of them undergoes editing again and again.

In the Preface to the 1985 edition of an English-Arabic

17) Galatians 1:8.
18) See Sura 6:34; 10:64.

Qur'an, the translators, Dr. Muhammad Taqi-ud-Din Al-Hilali and Dr. Muhammad Muhsin Khan, both professors of Arabic language in Saudi Arabia, wrote:

> Some additions, corrections and alterations have been made to improve the English translation and to bring the English interpretation very close to the correct and exact meanings of the Arabic text. As regards the old edition of this Book, nobody is allowed to reprint or to reproduce it after this new edition has been published.

The main reason why Muslims claim the Bible is corrupted is because it speaks of the deity of Christ. They say they cannot bow down to "the Man of Galilee" because Jesus was a created being just as Adam was, and is no more a son of God than Adam (Sura 3:59).

Let us accept that for the sake of the following argument. The Qur'an says in no less than eight places that when Adam was created, God commanded all angels to bow down and worship the man He had made:

> We said to the angels: "Prostrate yourselves before Adam." And they prostrated except Iblis (Satan), he refused and was proud and was one of the disbelievers.[19]

What made *Iblis* an unbeliever was his refusal to bow to Adam. In Suras 15 and 38, God released some curses

19) Sura 2:34 (Hilali and Khan); Suras 7:11ff; 15:29-35; 17:61-62; 18:50; 20:115ff and 38:71ff

on *Iblis* for this arrogance. But if Muslims were on earth at that time, would they too have bowed down to Adam? And would that not be un-Islamic? The Bible says Jesus is the last Adam (though not in the Islamic sense):

> And so it is written, The first man Adam
> became a living soul; the last Adam became
> a quickening (life-giving) spirit. The first
> man was of the earth, earthy; the second
> Man is the Lord from heaven.[20]

No honest Muslim can deny any of these Bible claims. Adam was dust. But according to the Qur'an, Jesus Christ is not dust but the Word of God (*khalimatu'llah*), and a Spirit from Him (*Ruhun minhu*). God is quoted in the Qur'an as speaking of Jesus as "Our Spirit" (Sura 21:91). We ask: Is God's own Spirit a separate entity or part of Him? And is this Spirit divine or not?

If the first Adam, mere dust, must be worshipped, even by angels, why not the last Adam, God's life-giving Son? With all humility, therefore, we say that if Muslims refuse to bow to the last Adam, they have joined forces of rebellion and arrogance with Iblis, and are under the same curse released on Satan. It is a simple logic.

Some Muslims say they actually believe in Jesus. But that is not really true. One may believe in a historical "Jesus," a man of Galilee, one of the prophets of God, a great teacher who spoke in parables, a good man who treated his neighbors right, produced bread and other miracles.

20) 1 Corinthians 15:45, 47.

It is possible to believe all this, yet miss the critical truth. The devil doesn't care if a man believes everything else in the Bible, as long as he rejects the Sonship of Jesus.

The Lord once asked His disciples, *"Whom do men say that I the Son of man am?"* The answer is very important because our salvation lies there. A Muslim would say, "He is one of the mightiest messengers of God; no more;" but there he misses it. Jesus is more than a prophet. If, as Christians, all we do is convince a Muslim that Jesus is a great prophet, we have achieved nothing.

Peter's answer was: *"Thou art the Christ, the Son of the living God"* (Matthew 16:13-16). Jesus said it took a revelation of God for Peter to know this in his heart and confess it.

A Muslim who has a problem in this regard should ask God to open his heart to understand this important truth. John said in his account of the Gospel:

> …that ye might believe that Jesus is the
> Christ, the Son of God; and that believing
> ye might have life through his name.[21]

Believing Jesus means believing in <u>His Name</u>, which means "Jehovah our salvation" or "our Saviour." So a Muslim who does not believe that Jesus is man's salvation cannot say he believes in Jesus. Salvation is in the belief in His name; and it is the Name that speaks of His Lordship. Scripture says:

> Believe on the Lord Jesus Christ, and thou
> shalt be saved."[22]

21) John 20:31.
22) Acts 16:31.

You don't just believe in "Jesus," but "The Lord Jesus Christ." That is, your Lord, and God's Christ. That is the simple faith that can do the supernatural work of changing the heart and making one right with God. The believing only means agreeing with God. Refusal simply means pride.

A Muslim has the choice to agree with God or depend on his limited reasoning and remain in his sins. What did Jesus say in that regard?

> ...if ye believe not that I am he, ye shall die in your sins."[23]

> For there are three that bear record in heaven, the Father, the Word, and the Holy Ghost: and these three are one...

> If we receive the witness of men, the witness of God is greater: for this is the witness of God which he hath testified of his Son. He that believeth on the Son of God hath the witness in himself:

> he that believeth not God hath made him a liar; because he believeth not the record that God gave of his Son.

> And this is the record, that God hath given to us eternal life, and this life is in his Son. He that hath the Son hath life; and he that hath not the Son of God hath not life."[24]

23) John 8:24.
24) 1 John 5:7, 9-12.

THE MUSLIM HEAVEN

CHAPTER SEVEN

A THOROUGH STUDY of the Qur'an shows that the Christian heaven is different from the Muslim paradise, despite the euphoria they both promise. In this chapter, we will compare these two places and see how this helps us identify Allah.

The Qur'an says there will be a lot of sexual activity in paradise.[1] The book talks of many virgins which no persons or angels have deflowered. They are "pure spouses" (Sura 3:15) and "wide-eyed *houri*"[2] There are companions with beautiful big and lustrous eyes, "maidens with swelling breasts."[3]

1) Sura 56:10-22, 35-38
2) A *houri* means "a voluptuously alluring woman or a nymph of the Muhammadan's paradise." Chambers 20th Century Dictionary.
See Suras 55:45-75; 37:48; 44:50-55
3) Sura 38:52; Sura 52:20

One *Hadith* says each Muslim (especially if he fought jihad very well on earth for the cause of Allah), will be entitled to 500 *houris*, 4,000 virgins and 8,000 non-virgins, making 12,000 women altogether, just for one person!

In another *Hadith*, Muhammad said:

> The lowliest of the inhabitants of paradise will be he who has eighty thousand (80,000) servants, seventy-two wives..."[4]

Many commentators believe these 80,000 "servants" will be females as they cannot see how so many men could be "serving" one man.

If all these are for "the lowliest of the inhabitants (Muslims)," what will be the share of the Chief Imams and Sheikhs? We do not know. Lest anyone should spiritualize or make a metaphor of this issue, Anas in the *Hadith* reported the Prophet of Islam as saying:

> In paradise, the believer will be given such power to conduct sexual intercourse." [5]

From this, we know the issue is not a metaphor.

MOTIVATION FOR SUICIDE BOMBING

The Western world is still willfully ignorant about the motivation for suicide bombers. In some cases, when a Palestinian Muslim kills himself in a suicide attack, the relatives celebrate his "paradise wedding" with their neighbors by distributing sweets and other things.

---

4) *Mishkat al Masabih*, Sh. M. Ashraf (1990) p. 1204.
5) Ibid. p. 1200.

On June 1, 2001, there was a suicide bombing by Sa'id Al-Hutari outside a pop house near the Dolphinarium in Tel Aviv killing 23 people, mostly teenage girls. On July 7, *Al Risala*, the Hamas" mouthpiece, published the written will of Al-Hitari the suicide bomber. He wrote:

> "I will turn my body into bombs that will
> hunt the sons of Zion, blast them, and
> burn their remains. Call out in joy, oh my
> mother; distribute sweets, oh my father and
> brothers; a wedding with "the black-eyed"
> awaits your son in Paradise."[6]

Palestinian Muslim, Nassim Abu "Aasi, who died while attempting to carry out an attack on Israel, was often asked why he was not married. His reply was always:

> Why should I relinquish "the black-eyed"
> to marry women of clay (i.e. flesh and
> blood)?[7]

Sheikh Abd Al-Salam Abu Shukheydem, Chief Mufti of the Palestinian Authority police force, mentioned "the black-eyed" as one of the rewards of an Islamic martyr, and a major motivation for their attacks. He said:

> From the moment the first drop of his
> blood is spilled, he does not feel the pain
> of his wounds and he is forgiven for all his
> sins; he sees his seat in Paradise; he is saved
> from the torment of the grave; he is saved

---

6) *Al-Risala* (Palestinian Authority), July 7, 2001.
7) Al-Hayat Al-Jadida (Palestinian Authority), September 11, 2001.

from the great horror of Judgment Day;
he marries "the black-eyed;" he vouches
for 70 of his family members; he gains
the crown of honor, the precious stone of
which is better than this entire world and
everything in it.[8]

The Israeli media reported the case of a suicide bomber
who was caught before he managed to carry out his mission.
He was wearing a towel as a loincloth to protect his genitals
for use in paradise. Author and journalist Muhammad Galal
Al-Kushk Kurum, wrote:

"In Paradise, a believer's penis is eternally
erect."[9]

One of the main reasons why young men join suicide
teams and die in cars and airplanes is their conviction that they
will open their eyes at the bosom of women in paradise!

MUHAMMAD'S EXAMPLE

It will be helpful to flash back to the life of the prophet,
Muhammad. Some traditions say he had 27 wives; some say
29. Others say 9, 11 and 13. But we know that there were
many, and new ones were acquired after nearly every war his
army fought. Later these women were kept in the harem.

Known wives included Aisha (Ayesha), Hafsa, Safia,
Sawda, Um Salama, Zainab (also spelled "Zaynab"), Mariam,
Ummu Habiba, Maymuna, Raihana, Juwayriyya and Safiyya.
Ali Dashti gave more names.

8) Al-Hayat Al-Jadida (Palestinian Authority), September 17, 1999.
9) Al-Quds Al-Arabi (London), 5/11/01 Al-Quds Al-Arabi (London), 5/11/01.

The Qur'an reveals the scope of the privileges of women Muhammad enjoyed:

> O Prophet (Muhammad)! Verily, We have made lawful to you your wives, to whom you have paid their Mahr (dower, or dowry), and those (captives or slaves) whom your right hand possesses - whom Allah has given to you, and the daughters of your (paternal uncles) and the daughters of your (paternal aunts) and the daughters of your (maternal uncles and the daughters of your (maternal aunts... who migrated (from Mecca) with you, and a believing woman if she offers herself to the Prophet, and the Prophet wishes to marry her; a privilege for you only, not for the (rest of) the believers...[10]

In spite of all the women Muhammad had, all his male children died young. He therefore adopted a boy, Zaid ibn Harithah, who grew up and was blessed with a charming young lady, Zainab. Unfortunately, she became too much of a temptation for the prophet.

One day, on a visit to Zaid's house, Muhammad saw Zainab not completely covered. Overwhelmed by her beauty, the prophet gasped: "Praise belongeth unto Allah, who turneth the hearts of men as he willeth."

Before long, arrangements were completed for Zaid to divorce Zainab so the prophet could marry her. At first,

10) Sura 33:50 (Hilali and Khan).

Muhammad feared what people would say if he seduced
Zainab. So he first showed he was not personally interested
in the lady. But Allah rebuked him for such seeming hypocrisy and fear:

> ...you said to him (Zaid)... "Keep your
> wife to yourself, and fear Allah." But you
> (Muhammad) did hide in yourself... that
> which Allah will make manifest, you did
> fear the people... whereas Allah had a better
> right that you should fear Him.[11]

In essence, he is saying: If I turned your heart toward the
beauty of Zaid's wife, why are you afraid of men in making
the right decision? Do you fear men more than me?

Muhammad therefore yielded to the will of Allah and
took Zainab to be his wife. No, the drama wasn't regarded
as a sin. Two revelations quickly came from Allah to justify
the action for posterity. One says:

> So when Zaid had accomplished his desire
> from her (i.e. divorced her), We gave her to
> you in marriage, so that (in future) there
> may be no difficulty to the believers in
> respect of (the marriage of) the wives of
> their adopted sons when the latter have no
> desire to keep them (i.e. they have divorced
> them). And Allah's commandment must
> be fulfilled.[12]

11) Sura 33:37 (Hilali and Khan).
12) Sura 33:37 (Hilali and Khan) et al.

Some modern Muslim writers have been sweating to explain this issue away. Some say her husband no longer wanted to keep her because Zainab was too proud of her beauty. Even if this were true, an Apostle of Jesus Christ or a genuine Pastor would have taught his converts the Godly principles of a successful marriage instead of taking over the wife to "settle the matter."[13]

Some apologists say Zaid willingly divorced Zainab and gave her to the Prophet of his own volition and with all his heart; and according to the Qur'an, he had no more desire to keep her.

But hardly could Zaid have *willingly* relinquished his newly-wedded darling to somebody else. And hardly could Zainab have willingly abandoned her youthful, energetic husband for an over 50-year-old. But the young couple had no choice. Zaid was being respectful. He did not want to show his disappointment about the man he had grown up to regard as his father, and was so nice to him since childhood.

Moreover, since Muhammad insisted that his claim over Zaid's wife was the will and decree of Allah (and he was the one receiving the revelations), Zaid could do nothing but submit. (Submission to the will of Allah is what makes a good Muslim). Muhammad issued a warning on anybody's reaction to this matter:

> It is not fitting for a Believer, man or woman, when a matter has been decided by Allah and His Messenger to have any

13) Ephesians 5:22-33; Colossians 3:18-19.

> option about their decision: if any one
> disobeys Allah and His Messenger, he is
> indeed on a clearly wrong path.[14]

Did Muhammad actually have such a revelation? Muslims say, yes. Was it from Allah? They say, yes. One wonders then who this Allah is that makes such a commandment and "turneth the hearts of men" to do such a thing. Jesus Christ has a clear stand on this kind of situation:

> But I say unto you, That whosoever shall
> put away his wife, saving for the cause of
> fornication, causeth her to commit adul-
> tery: and <u>whosoever</u> shall marry her that
> is divorced committeth adultery.[15]

If Muhammad had not claimed that the Allah of the Qur'an is the God of the Bible, we would not have bothered with this. It is that claim that we find problematic.

King David of Israel fell into an almost similar temptation. But he never justified his action; and God never condoned it. David was punished for it. In the revelation that came to him through Nathan, God said:

> Now therefore, the sword shall never
> depart from thine house, because thou
> hast despised me and has taken the wife
> of Uriah the Hittite to be thy own.[16]

The sword has not departed from the house of David (Israel) until today. God said that by taking Uriah's wife,

14) Sura 33:36 (Yusuf Ali). See Sahih Al-Bukhari, *Hadith* No. 384, Vol. 9.
15) Matthew 5:32.
16) 2 Samuel 12:10.

David was despising Him who has given every man his own wife. That is why we do not believe that the God of the Bible would lead Muhammad to take somebody else's wife —the wife of his own adopted son.

Apart from the four wives that Muslims are allowed to have, Allah says in Sura 4:24ff that they are also free to take their slave girls or housemaids as wives. In Saudi Arabia and many Gulf countries today, many Filipino and Indian girls who serve as housemaids are easy prey. Little wonder that the Muslim paradise is so laced with sexual content, given the example of its prophet.

MUT'AH: DIVINE PROSTITUTION?

If he is a traveler, a tourist or a pilgrim, the faithful Muslim may have some other temporary "wives" at strategic places wherever he lodges. This "marriage" is known as *mut'ah* or the Law of Desire. The word *mut'ah* means "desire" or "pleasure." *Mut'ah* marriage may last for one hour or as long as the man desires.

Under Ayatollah Khomeini, Iran was regarded by some Muslims worldwide as an example of the kingdom of Allah on earth. Since Sharia, the Islamic legal system, became fully operational in Iran in 1979, *mut'ah* has been revitalized. Many Iranian women (most of them divorcees) are engaged in *mut'ah* for economic sustenance.

According to a research done by an Iranian woman, Shahla Haeri,[17] *mut'ah* flourishes in Iran and Egypt today.

17) Haeri, Shahla, *Law of Desire*. I.B. Taurus & Co., Ltd, 110 Gloucester Aven., London.

Some Islamic scholars in Iran believe that one is even free to contract many *mut'ahs* at the same time —apart from the four wives and slave girls or house-helps the Muslim man may have at home.

Historian Burkhardt pointed out that *mut'ah* was already prevalent in Arabia before Muhammad started preaching. The custom was that a host would offer one of his female relatives to his guest for the night. The "marriage" ended the following morning or whenever the guest left.

When the practice became fully developed in Islam, it became an arrangement between a man and an unmarried woman, preferably a virgin, divorcee or widow. The partners agree in advance how long the relationship shall last and the amount of money to be paid by the man.

Witnesses are not required nor parents involved; the marriage need not be registered. At the end of the agreed time, the temporary "spouses" part without any formality or divorce ceremony.

After separation, the woman must abstain from sex for two months to know who fathered the child that may result. This practice is common especially among tourists, pilgrims and visitors. With such provision, one does not have to travel with one's wife to avoid adultery.

A modern Muslim who grew up or was educated in America or Europe may contend that *mut'ah* is just an invention of some weak Iranian or Egyptian men and not an approved practice of the prophet of Islam. But commenting on Sura 4:24, Al-Razi, one of the greatest Islamic thinkers says:

Muta'ah marriage involved a man *hiring* a woman for a specific amount of money, for a certain period of time, *to have sex* with her. The scholars agree that this Mut'ah marriage was authorized in the beginning of Islam. It is reported that when the Prophet came to Mecca to perform "Omrah, the women of Mecca dressed up and adorned themselves. The Companions (that is, the followers of Muhammad) complained to the Prophet that they had not had sex for a long time, so he said to them: "enjoy these women."

In the *Hadith* Mishkat-ul-Masabih, we read:

Ibn Masu'd reported: We were fighting along with Messenger of Allah while (our) wives were not with us. We said: shall we not undergo castration? The Holy Prophet forbade us from that. Afterwards he made lawful Mut'ah Marriage. So all of us married a woman for a fixed term in exchange for a cloth. Afterwards Abdullah (i.e. servant of Allah, Muhammad) recited: O those who believe! Do not make unlawful the good things which Allah has made for you.[18]

That means the revelation of Allah in Sura 5:87 and quoted in that *Hadith* came to give a divine approval on *Mut'ah*.[19]

18) Sura 5:87; *Mishkat ul Masabih*, Book 2, *Hadith* #115.
19) See also the *Hadith* of Sahih Bukhari, 6:139 and 7:13o; and the *Hadith* of

If Allah gave these instructions through Muhammad, we need to ask if Allah is the same God that reveals Himself in the Bible. When foreign journalists complain every year of prostitution in Mecca during the *hajj*, it is because they do not understand what goes on.

To the Christian, all this nullifies God's clear injunction: *"Thou shalt not commit adultery."* To a Muslim, such a commandment is vague. *Mut'ah* makes the words "adultery" "fornication" and "prostitution" very difficult to define.

It also makes a mockery of the Islamic legal system called *Sharia,* which stipulates that an adulterer or fornicator be executed. If two people are caught and say they were only doing *mut'ah,* how would the jurists disprove them?

WIFE BEATING

A husband has permission from Allah in Sura 4:34 to beat up his wife if she misbehaves after having been admonished. Or he may refuse to move close to her for any time as a punishment (since he has others inside or outside).

By comparing this with what the God of the Bible commands the husband-wife relationship to be,[20] we have a problem believing that the Allah speaking in the Qur'an is the same God whose Word we have in the Bible.

NO FORGIVENESS

The woman seems to be always at the receiving end of Allah's punishment of immorality. In practice, forgiveness

---

Sahih Muslim, 8:3243.
20) See Ephesians 5:25-33, Colossians 3:19 and 1 Corinthians 7:5.

is far from Allah. In the *Hadith* Sahih Muslim, we read of a woman who confessed to Muhammad her unfaithfulness to her husband, which had led to pregnancy:

> Muhammad then called her master (husband) and said: Treat her well, and when she delivers, bring her to me." He did accordingly. Then Allah's Apostle pronounced judgment about her and her clothes were tied around her and then he commanded and she was stoned to death."[21]

One person cannot commit adultery. Where was the man who impregnated the lady? Women in a democratic society who flirt with Islam may not know the full implications of their curiosity. It is as if men do not commit immorality. Allah tells his prophet:

> And those of your <u>women</u> who commit illegal sexual intercourse, take the evidence of four witnesses from amongst you against them; and if they testify, confine them (i.e. women) to houses until death comes to them or Allah ordains for them some (other) way."[22]

When a woman commits "illegal sexual intercourse," she must be detained in a room until she dies or until the best way of killing her is determined by the Islamic authorities. But Allah does not tell us what should be done to the man who commits "illegal sexual intercourse" with the woman.

21) *Hadith* #4207.
22) Sura 4:15 (Hilali and Khan).

RIVERS OF WINE IN ISLAMIC PARADISE

With this background of marital life in Islam, it is perhaps not surprising that the Islamic paradise should be full of "women affairs." But apart from the unlimited honeymoons of Muhammad's paradise, there are also "rivers of wine" flowing in that heaven.[23] This must be a wonderful and promising paradise for all unrepentant winebibbers and beer soakers.

Because of Sura 5:93, wine is forbidden in some Islamic countries. Some people have seen this as a contradiction. But abstinence here may simply be to prepare our throats for the Great Beyond. One *Hadith* says:

> If you want to enjoy wine in the hereafter,
> abstain from it here.

In *Mishkat al Masabih* (1990), Muhammad said:

> He who drinks wine in this world and
> dies when he is addicted to it, not having
> repented, will not drink it in the next.

With all the drinking sprees and women affairs in the Islamic heaven, observers have wondered if Allah would not have a problem getting the attention of Muslims to worship him in that paradise. They have done enough worship on earth. Now, it is time for sensuous enjoyment unlimited.

Someone asks, "Will all these orgies and profligacy be done in the presence of Allah in heaven?" Who knows? The whole Qur'an contains no description of Allah being present in paradise.

23) Suras 47:15; 76: 5, 21; 83:25-29.

Sol, a Muslim who worshipped a "God" he did not know goes to a paradise where he still will not know or see that God or His glory.

Again, the Bible disagrees. Jesus said, *"Blessed are the pure in heart, for they shall see God"* (Matthew 5:8). If anyone dies *in* his sins without being forgiven, no matter what religion he had on earth, he will not be in the Heaven of God, but will be consigned to Hell.

Jesus told a very religious woman:

> Ye (Samaritans) worship ye know not what: we know what we worship. For salvation is of the Jews."[24]

To those who believe in Him, the Lord said:

> Let not your heart be troubled: ye believe in God, believe also in me. In my Father's house are many mansions: if it were not so, I would have told you. I go to prepare a place for you.
>
> And if I go and prepare a place for you, I will come again, and receive you unto myself; that where I am, there ye may be also. And whither I go ye know, and the way ye know."
>
> Thomas said to him, "Lord, we know not whither thou goest; and how can we know the way?"

24) John 4:22.

> Jesus saith unto him, "I am the way, the
> truth, and the life: no man cometh unto
> the Father but by me."[25]

The Heaven of the Christian is where Jesus is. We will
see Him with the Father in glory. The Bible says "...*we shall
see him as he is*."[26]

The "rivers of wine" issue has embarrassed a few thought-
ful Muslim exegetes. But they are smart guys! In an attempt
to explain this, some say the wine is not alcoholic, (for they
could not imagine how such a heaven could be).

One of them says even if the rivers are alcoholic, that is
why a committed Muslim should not drink wine or beer on
earth, since there will be enough of that in their heaven.

In the *Hadith* quoted earlier, Muhammad said any one
addicted to wine here on earth will not drink "it" in paradise.
That means the wine that can be addicted to on earth will
be available in paradise.

But the Bible says:

> "Now the works (practices) of the flesh are
> manifest, which are these; Adultery, fornica-
> tion, uncleanness, lasciviousness,
>
> Idolatry, witchcraft, hatred, variance, emu-
> lations, wrath, strife, seditions, heresies,
>
> Envyings, murders, drunkenness, revel-
> lings, and such like: of the which I tell you
> before, as I have also told you in time past,

25) John 14:1-6.
26) 1 John 3:2; Revelation 22:3-4.

> that they which do such things shall NOT
> inherit the Kingdom of God."[27]

Since these sinful behaviors are characteristic of those who reject Christ, it seems unlikely that they would be allowed once you arrived. The joy of the Christian heaven is not in drinking and sex:

> For the kingdom of God is not meat and
> drink; but righteousness, and peace, and
> joy in the Holy Ghost."[28]

Surely, during the "Marriage Supper of the Lamb" Jesus will share the juice of the fruit of the vine with all His people (Matthew 26:26-29). It is the common grape or vine juice He produced during the Marriage at Cana in Galilee, and the one He took with bread (as with tea) during the Last Supper with the disciples. It is the common health drink of the Jews (1 Timothy 5:23).

But there is nothing like "rivers of wine" in Jesus' heaven. He promises what John saw in his revelation —a "pure river of the water of life" (Revelation 21:6-8; 22:1-2). We can be sure that this "water of life" does not mean wine or any liquor. The Christian heaven is more wonderful than imaginable.

Wine and women may be the most exciting and thrilling things Muhammad could imagine. But the experiences of the redeemed of the Lord will be more titillating than sex. The joy of heaven is not of the earth, and so no human expressions can adequately describe it. The Bible says:

27) Galatians 5:19-21.
28) Romans 14:17.

> But as it is written, Eye hath not seen, nor
> ear heard, neither have entered into the
> heart of man the things which God hath
> prepared for them that love Him.[29]

John saw only a glimpse of it in the book of Revelation
and could describe only as far as he could as a human being.
In Matthew 22:30, Jesus says the very opposite of what
Muhammad says about heaven. We may ask if this Allah who
"revealed" the doctrine to Muhammad is the same God from
whom Jesus said He received His messages. Jesus said: "

> I have not spoken of myself; but the Father
> which sent me..., whatsoever I speak there-
> fore, even as the Father said unto me, so
> I speak.[30]

Who is "the Father?"

THE MARRIAGE OF THE LAMB

The Bible indeed talks of "The Marriage Supper of the
Lamb" that will take place in heaven (Revelation 19:7-8).
This event has nothing to do with the sex acts of the Muham-
madan paradise or "Gardens of Retreat." The Marriage of
the Lamb is not between individuals. It is the joining of the
Lord Jesus Christ (the Lamb of God) and His Church.

The Church of God, which is the body of all who have
been "called out" of the world to reign with Him, is often
referred to in Scripture as "the Bride" (not Brides). The metaphor of "Bride-Bridegroom" is used to show the precious-

29) 1 Corinthians 2:9.
30) John 12:49-50.

ness of the Church of Christ, His love for "her," how He cherishes "her," and the preparations being made by Him to receive "her" into glory in "my Father's house" (Read Ephesians 5:25-32).

But Allah says, "We shall espouse them (Muslims) to wide eyed *houris.*"[31] For those who believe in heavenly weddings, Jesus says:

> Ye do err, not knowing the Scriptures,
> nor the power of God. For in the resur-
> rection they neither marry nor are given
> in marriage, but are as angels of God in
> heaven.[32]

Muslim historians have pointed out that life in the pre-Islamic Arabia was a life of "the three w's" —wine, women and war.[33] It is therefore not surprising that the new religion should be preferable to the Gospel of Christ. Here they could war to even gain paradise; they could have many women (especially as booty of war); and they could expect more women and free wine when they die. Who would not opt for that?

We need to realize this is a major motivation for Islamic suicide bombings.

31) Sura 44:54; Sura 52:20; Sura 55:70 (A.J. Arberry).
32) Matthew 22:29-30; Mark 12:24-25.
33) Ebrahim, *Anecdotes From Islam.*

ALLAH MISLEADS TO HELL

CHAPTER EIGHT

SEVERAL VERSES in the Qur'an say Allah can mislead a person away from the way of salvation if he chooses:

> …Allah leads astray whom He will and guides whom He will.[1]

> …Allah misleads whom He wills and guides whom He wills. And He is the All-Mighty, the All-Wise.[2]

Though Allah led you astray, on the judgment day, he can still call you to account for any evil you did:

> And had Allah willed, He could have made

1) Sura 74:31 (Hilali and Khan).
2) Sura 14:4 (Hilali and Khan). In a desperate attempt to rescue Islam from the embarrassment of these verses, Yusuf Ali deliberately tried to change these areas. But textual comparison with other translations exposes his slyness.

you (all) one nation, but He sends astray
whom He wills and guides whom He wills.
But you shall certainly be called to account
for what you used to do.[3]

The Qur'an warns that nobody should lead a person to
the way of salvation who has been led astray by Allah:

Do you want to guide him whom Allah has
made to go astray? And he whom Allah has
made to go astray, you will never find for
him any way (of guidance).[4]

But Jesus said:

I am the light of the world: he that fol-
loweth me shall not walk in darkness, but
shall have the light of life.[5]

Christians follow the God and Father of Jesus Christ,
and He can never lead us astray to Hell. He is a God...

Who will have all men to be saved, and
come unto the knowledge of the truth.[6]

That is why He created the plan of salvation... because
of His great love for us. An Allah who delights in leading
men to hell fire cannot be that LORD. Allah says:

Many are the Jinns and men we have made
for Hell.[7]

But the good God in the Bible did not make anybody

3) Sura 16:93 (Hilali and Khan).
4) Sura 4:88 (Hilali and Khan).
5) John 8:12.
6) 1 Timothy 2:4; 2 Peter 3:9.
7) Sura 7:179 (Yusuf Ali).

for hell; neither did He create hell for man. Jesus said hell was created for Satan and his angels (Matthew 25:41).

Many people will be in hell, not because it was made for them, but because they followed Satan and his demonic teachings. Even the evil spirits that will be turned to hell were not created to go there. The Bible says *"In the beginning, God created the heaven and the earth."*[8]

The devil rebelled against God and persuaded many other *jinns* to rebel with him, so they will all be in hell together.

The devil continues to lead man into sin, false religions and all sorts of wickedness today so they will accompany him in hell. So when we read, "Many are the *Jinns* and men we have made for Hell," it is easy to recognize that this is not the voice of the God of the Bible.

ALL BLACK PEOPLE FOR HELL?

Today, when Muslims come to America and South Africa they tell the Blacks that they should reject Christianity as the "White man's religion," and accept Islam, which they say is an international brotherhood.

That is why Islam is being embraced mostly by the Blacks in the United States. In Europe, Islam's message is different.

Is Islam really an international brotherhood? In an Islamic tradition, Muhammad says Allah destined all Black people for hell fire, while the Whites are destined for heaven:

The holy prophet said: Allah created Adam.

8) Genesis 1:1.

> Then He stroke his right shoulder and took
> out a white race as if they were seeds, and
> He stroke his left shoulder and took out a
> black race as if they were coals.

> Then He said to those who were on his right
> side: Towards paradise and I don't care. He
> said to those who were on his left shoulder:
> Towards hell and I don't care.[9]

WILL ALL MUSLIMS GO TO HELL?

The Qur'an makes a shocking but clear statement that
ALL Muslims will go to hell but will be rescued, while the
kafirun (unbelievers) will remain in hell:

> There is not one of you but will pass over
> it (Hell); this is with your Lord; a Decree
> which must be accomplished. Then We
> shall save those who use to fear Allah and
> were dutiful to Him. And We shall leave
> the wrongdoers therein (humbled) to their
> knees (in Hell).[10]

In case you doubt the rendering of these verses, let us
quote N.J. Dawood's translation:

> There is not one of you who shall not pass
> through the confines of hell…[11]

J.M. Rodwell's translation (1950 edition) renders it:

9) *Mishkat-ul-Masabih,* Vol. III, p. 117. Note: Today, even Arabs are not
regarded by Europeans as White men.
10) Sura 19:71-72 (Hilali and Khan).
11) Qur'an, Penguin Books Ltd., 1959.

> No one there is of you who shall not go
> down into it…"

The popular Pickthall's translation says:

> There is not one of you but shall approach
> it. That is a fixed ordinance of thy Lord.
> Then We shall rescue those who are kept
> from evil, and leave the evil-doers crouch-
> ing there.[12]

In a later edition, Pickthall recasts the second sentence:

> That is a fixed decree of thy Lord.

Professor A.J. Arberry's translation has it as:

> …We[13] shall parade them about Gehenna
> (Hell Fire) hobbling on their knees. Then we
> shall pluck forth from those most deserving
> to burn there. Not one of you there is, but
> he shall go down to it; that for thy Lord is a
> thing decreed, determined. Then We shall
> deliver those that were god fearing; and the
> evildoers We shall leave there, hobbling on
> their knees." every party whichever of them
> was the most hardened…; then We shall
> know very well (from verse 69).

Commenting on Sura 42:13, Drs. Muhammad Al-Hilali
and Muhsin Khan quote Muhammad:

> "Jews will be divided into 71 religious sects

12) *The Meaning of the Glorious Koran*, New York, 1954.
13) "We" indicates that Allah will also be in hell. This is significant in
identifying this Allah. God Almighty is in heaven and will never be in hell.

and the Christians will be divided into 72
religious sects and this nation (Muslims)
will be divided into 73 religious sects —all
in Hell, except one." It is in that context
that we can understand Sura 19:68-69:

…We (Allah) shall gather them (all these
people) together and also the devils (with
them); then We shall bring them round Hell
on their knees. Then indeed We shall drag
out from every sect all those who were worst
in obstinate rebellion against the Beneficent
(Allah).[14]

Devout Muslims will stay in hell until Allah rescues them
on the Day of Judgment. Meanwhile, millions of Muslims
have died since Islam started. The Day of Judgment has not
come yet. Where are these millions? If this Day does not
come in the next one thousand years, they will remain there,
and millions more will join them.

The Qur'an reveals that being a Muslim qualifies a man
for hell; and real "salvation" comes only after one is in hell.
But the Bible says that no one can be rescued from hell:

For if the word spoken by angels was steadfast (binding) and every transgression and
disobedience received a just recompense
(punishment)…, how shall we escape if
we neglect so great salvation."[15]

14) Hilali and Khan translation.
15) Hebrews 2:2-3.

Compare Allah's way of "salvation" with that of Jesus:

> There is therefore now NO condemnation
> to them which are in Christ Jesus…"[16]

Even Muhammad did not know for sure if he was in the sect (party) that will be "plucked forth" from hell. The *Hadith* reports:

> I heard the Messenger of Allah say, "Verily
> the Almighty and Glorious Allah caught
> one party with His right hand and another
> with another hand, and said: "This is for
> this, and this is for this, and I don't care."
> I don't know in which of the two parties
> I am."[17]

This is corroborated in the Qur'an, where Allah tells Muhammad to:

> Say: I am no bringer of new-fangled doc-
> trine among the messengers, nor do I know
> what will be done with me or with you.
> I follow but that which is revealed to me
> by inspiration; I am but a Warner open
> and clear.[18]

The only person assured of direct entry to paradise at death is the one who dies on the battleground while fighting the Islamic holy war (*jihad*). All others will enter hell, and be "plucked forth" on the Day of Judgment.

16) Romans 8:1.
17*) Mishakt-ul-Masabih*, Vol. 3, Cha. 33:32 (455W). Cited in Nehls, G. *Destination Unknown*, Life Challenge, Nairobi (1992) p. 3.
18) Sura 46:9 (Yusuf Ali).

Unfortunately, Muhammad did not die on the battle-ground. Some Islamic historians say he died of pneumonia. Some say he died of food poisoning from a Jewish woman he forced to marry him after killing her husband in a war.

Therefore, Islamic terrorism is not bravery, or evidence of the greatness of Islam. Terrorism is the evidence of the hope-lessness of the religion. The Muslim's only hope of paradise is to die while fighting the perceived enemy of Islam.

The "good news" of Islam is if you enter a car or bus with bombs and die along with your "enemies," your eyes will open in paradise to see thousands of celestial women with rivers of wine flowing all around you. Muhammad said:

> To fall a martyr in the cause of Allah (Jihad) atones for everything except a debt… Six rewards are conferred on a martyr by Allah." The first, is that, "he is forgiven immediately and his abode in paradise is shown him." The fifth: "Seventy-two celestial brides will be given to him in marriage.[19]

What if the martyr is a lady? How many husbands will she be entitled to? Even if there were no Palestinian question and no America, there would still be jihadists who wanted to die in the cause of spreading or defending their religion. Many in the West do not understand this issue.

God said, *"Have not I held my peace even of old, and thou fearest me not?"* (Isaiah 57:11b). And Jesus said:

19) A tradition quoted in Maulana Mohammad Manzoor Nomani, *What is Islam* (Series No. 21). Nadwatul (India): Islamic Research and Publications, 1979, p. 94.

> For ye compass sea and land (travel overseas)
> to make (win) one proselyte (convert), and
> when he is made, ye make him twofold more
> the child of hell than yourselves,"

> If therefore the light in thee be darkness,
> how great is that darkness!"[20]

ALLAH AND THE HOPE OF SINNERS

A sinner, if he has any sense of logic, will be disappointed if he reads the Qur'an seeking a sure and certain hope of salvation and rest for his soul. According to the Qur'an, Allah has already decided not to save some people. Hear him:

> Verily, those who disbelieve, it is the same
> to them whether you warn them or do not
> warn them, they will not believe. Allah has
> set a seal on their hearts and on their hear-
> ings, and on their eyes there is a covering.
> Theirs will be a great torment.[21]

"Allah does not love the unbelievers"[22] or sinners.[23] He loves only those who love him[24] and those who fight wars to spread Islam.[25] He loves the just, the righteous, the kind, and those who do good and are neat and clean.[26] It is not easy to understand who this Allah is. It is recorded:

20) Matthew 23:15b; Matthew 6:23b.
21) Sura 2:6-7 (Hilali and Khan).
22) Sura 3:32 (Shakir).
23) Suras 2:190, 276; 3:140; 6:141; 42:40; 7:31,55, plus several other verses.
24) Suras 3:31; 5:57.
25) Sura 61:4.
26) Suras 5:14, 45; 49:9; 60:8; 2:222; 9:108.

> Verily, the almighty and Glorious Allah
> finished five things for every man of His cre-
> ation: his fixed term, <u>his action</u>, his resting
> place, his movement and his provision.[27]

That is to say Allah directs every man in whatever he does or becomes in life —good or evil. Those who are ungrateful have been created so by Allah, yet Allah does not love them for being so (Suras 100:6; 2:276).

Allah does not love the impatient, but he has created man to be impatient (Sura 70:19). Allah does not love the stingy, but he has created all men stingy.[28]

Allah does not love those who exult in riches,[29] yet he created every man "violent" in his love of wealth.[30] (If this is the case, where do the affluent Arab kings and princes stand before Allah?)

There is no clear-cut principle of justice by which Allah will judge Muslims. He says:

> And had Allah willed, He could have made
> you (all) one nation, but He sends astray
> whom He wills and guides whom He wills.
> But you shall certainly be called to account
> for what you used to do.[31]

That is, if you sin, Allah must have led you to do it. Yet he will throw you into hell when you die.

---

27) *Mishkat*, Vol. 3, p. 118, p. 30 (1990).
28) Suras 70:21; 17:100.
29) Sura 28:76.
30) Sura 100:8.
31) Sura 16:93 (Hilali and Khan).

In the *Hadith*, Muhammad says:

> Verily Allah has fixed the very portion of
> adultery which a man will indulge in, and
> which he of necessity must commit.[32]

Strange! This is different from the God of the Bible. The
Bible declares, *"For all have sinned and come short of the glory
of God"* (Romans 3:23).

But here is the good news of Jesus Christ:

> For God so loved the world (sinners), that
> He gave His only begotten Son, that who-
> soever believeth in him should not perish,
> but have everlasting life.

> For God sent not his Son into the world
> to condemn the world; but that the world
> through him might be saved. He that
> believeth on him is not condemned…[33]

The God of the Bible does not love us because we are
good. He loves us despite our sins, and therefore made a
provision to save us from the power of sin and to forgive
the sins we have committed.

The Bible says:

> But God commendeth (demonstrates) his
> love toward us, in that, while we were yet
> sinners, Christ died for us.[34]

32) *Sahih Muslim*, Sh. M. Ashraf, Lahore (1975) Vol. iv, pp. 1396-8. See also
Mishkat al Masabih Vol 3. Chapter 32:16 as reported by Abu Hurara and
Mishkat, Vol. 3, p. 103.
33) John 3:16-18a.
34) Romans 5:8.

Jesus said:

> Greater love hath no man than this, that a
> man lay down his life for his friends (sin-
> ners).[35]

We call on anyone, any sinner, any Muslim who needs love, truth and a reliable plan of salvation to compare the God of the Bible with whatever god you now believe in.

Each chapter of the Qur'an begins with the statement: "In the name of Allah, the most compassionate and merciful." But ask Muslims what Allah has done about their sins and they can only answer, "Maybe Allah will forgive me, maybe he will not. I will not know until I die and my good works are weighed against my evil works."

Christians are assured before they die that they are saved by the grace of God. In God's compassion, because He knows man's inability to fulfill the law, He came down to fulfill the law Himself in a Person (Matthew 5:17). All the punishment a sinner deserves is met in that Person, so that *"by the obedience of one shall many be made righteous."* (Roman 5:19).

God offers this assurance freely. That is why Christians believe God is "most compassionate and merciful."

Allah calls himself "most merciful;" yet he is determined to "fill the hell with mankind and *jinns* together" as a "fixed ordinance."

Christianity is positive and not fatalistic. The Christian believes the compassion of God is embodied in Jesus Christ, so anyone who has Jesus has all the fullness of God's love.

35) John 15:13.

CAN WE HANG OUR ETERNAL DESTINY ON THE WORDS OF ALLAH?

Let Allah speak for himself in the Qur'an:

> When We (Allah) substitute (or change) one revelation (or Verse) for another, - and Allah knows best what He reveals, - they say, "Thou art a forger": but most of them understand not.[36]

Sensible Arabs cannot understand how Allah could bring a new revelation today and then change it tomorrow. The Qur'an says:

> Allah blots out what He wills and confirms (what He wills)…[37]

In Sura 2:106, Allah says:

> Nothing of our revelation (even a single verse) do we abrogate or cause to be forgotten, but we bring (in place) one better or like thereof. Knowest thou not that Allah is Able to do all things?[38]

Revealing one thing today, and changing or denying it tomorrow is not the character of the God of the Bible.

ALLAH AND WASHING AWAY SIN

> O ye who believe! when ye prepare for prayer, wash your faces, and your hands (and arms) to the elbows; Rub your heads

36) Sura 16:101 (Yusuf Ali).
37 Sura 13:39 (Hilali and Khan).
38) Pickthall translation.

(with water); and (wash) your feet to the ankles."[39]

This is called Ablution (*wud'u*). Its purpose is to make the Muslim pure in the sight of Allah when praying. The Qur'an says Muslims who do not have water (e.g. travelers) should...

> ...take for yourselves clean sand or earth,
> and rub therewith your faces and hands.[40]
> For Allah doth blot out sins and forgive
> again and again.

A former devoted Muslim told me that even though he was a respected Chartered Accountant who studied in England, he still had to rub his face with sand when he was a Muslim. Though he is no longer a Muslim, he is still annoyed that he ever did such a thing.

The speaker in the Qur'an does not have the right perspective on sin. He does not know how serious sin is in the sight of God to suggest that washing your teeth, nose, ears and limbs with water or sand can purify a person so he can stand before a holy God.

Christians believe in personal cleanliness; but we do not believe that "cleanliness is godliness or next to godliness." That is a lie of the devil! Hygiene does not move you an inch closer to Almighty God. You can be a neat thief, or a clean, perfumed prostitute. The Psalmist says:

Who can ascend into the hill of the LORD?

39) Sura 5:6 (Yusuf Ali).
40) Sura 4:43 (Yusuf Ali). See also Sura 5:7 (Yusuf Ali).

> or who shall stand in His holy place? He that
> hath clean hands and a pure heart…"[41]

The "clean hands" here does not mean hands washed with water. Sins done with the hands are what make them unclean, not physical dirt. God makes this clear when He says:

> For though thou wash thee with nitre (soda), and take thee much soap, yet thine iniquity is marked before me, saith the Lord GOD.[42]

> For your hands are defiled with blood, and your fingers with iniquity; your lips have spoken lies, your tongue hath muttered perverseness.

> None calleth for justice, nor any pleadeth for truth: they trust in vanity, and speak lies; they conceive mischief, and bring forth iniquity.

> They hatch cockatrice' eggs, and weave the spider's web: he that eateth of their eggs dieth, and that which is crushed breaketh out into a viper. Their webs shall not become garments, neither shall they cover themselves with their works: their works are works of iniquity, and the act of violence is in their hands.

> Their feet run to evil, and they make haste

41) Psalm 24:3-4.
42) Jeremiah 2:22.

> to shed innocent blood: their thoughts are
> thoughts of iniquity; wasting and destruc-
> tion are in their paths.
>
> The way of peace they know not; and there
> is no judgment in their goings: they have
> made them crooked paths: whosoever goeth
> therein shall not know peace.[43]

A bath in the Zamzam well in Mecca cannot cleanse them. A billion barrels of Arabian perfumes cannot sweeten their hands stained with the blood of the people they have slaughtered or sponsored to do so.

Some of them may not participate in violence, but they morally support those who do. The blood of the children of God and all the innocent not only remains on the hands of all their enemies, but also cries to God daily, saying:

> How long, O Lord, holy and true, dost
> thou not judge and avenge our blood on
> them...?[44]

The question of sin and redemption should be the central issue in any religion; but the devil has created in Islam a religion without a redeemer, worship without a washing away of sin, and no definite plan of salvation.

43) Isaiah 59:3-8.
44) Revelation 6:10; Deuteronomy 32:43.

IS ISLAM THE RELIGION OF ADAM?

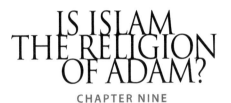

CHAPTER NINE

ACCORDING TO Islamic teaching, Islam did not begin with Muhammad. The Qur'an claims it was the religion of Adam, Noah, Ishmael, and all the prophets of God, including Jesus Christ before His crucifixion. Here, we examine Islam's identification with Adam and Jesus Christ.

We know that Adam was the first man. God did not give him a religion and he was not a prophet. God gave him only one commandment, to not eat the fruit from one particular tree. There is no religion in that.

But no sooner had Adam received it than he disobeyed it by listening to the voice of someone who promised that he and his wife could be "like God" —the very thing this being wanted and which caused him to lose his position in heaven (Isaiah 14:12-15).

Adam, on the advice of this crafty being, ate the fruit of the one forbidden tree.

God drove Adam from Eden, and he spent most of his life *outside Eden*. If he ever practiced any religion it must have been done outside the Garden of Eden. With his newly acquired "knowledge of good and evil," Adam tried to cover the shame of his sin with fig leaves. God proved he was foolish, and clothed him with *"coats of skins."* (Genesis 3:21).

But the descendants of Adam and Eve became so depraved that within a few generations, *"...every imagination of the thoughts of his heart was **only evil** continually"* (Genesis 6:5). All the good in man, all his righteousness was, in the sight of God, *"as filthy rags"* (Isaiah 64:6).

An animal had to be killed by God before Adam could be properly covered —an innocent animal, possibly a lamb, for its skin is more beautiful for covering than that of other animals. In the New Testament, we read:

> For Christ also hath once suffered for sins,
> the just for the unjust.... For He (God)
> hath made Him (Christ) to be sin for us,
> who knew no sin; that we might be made
> the righteousness of God."[1]

A sinless Christ died so those who acknowledge Him and His suffering might be clothed with <u>His</u> righteousness.

The religion inherited from Adam, then, tries to cloth oneself with man-made works of righteousness. But the good news is that God has a way of, not covering man's sins, but

1) 1 Peter 3:18; 2 Corinthians. 5:21.

washing them away once and for all. Any religion outside the redemptive work of Christ is a fig-leaf religion.

John the Baptist saw Jesus and prophetically declared: *"Behold, the Lamb of God which taketh away the sin of the world"* (John 1:29).

We know that man is a sinner because he sins. But conversely, he sins because he is a sinner. Every man came from Adam. If Adam had died at the age of six months, we would all have died in him. We would not be here today. This means we were in Adam when he was sinning. We became small Adams, small sinners, small rebels.

Therefore, man is born as a sinner. The egg is a sinner; the fertilizer is a sinner. (Psalm 58:3; 51:5). Man's condition is worsened if he finds a god that approves of his wickedness and promises a sensuous heaven as a reward.

Therefore, before a person can be right with the God of the Bible, his sins must be forgiven and blotted out. This is the work of the Blood that Christ shed on the Cross (Ephesians 2:14-16). By that, "old things are passed away," and "all things are become new." (2 Corinthians 5:17).

If Muslims maintain that the religion of Adam was Islam, then we would do well to probe the giver of that religion. Islam means submission, and Adam, indeed submitted. But he did not submit to the real God. He submitted to and obeyed the devil. If this is the same Allah of Muhammad, what then are Muslims telling us?

Another doctrine to examine is the claim by Muslims that Jesus Christ practiced Islam before His crucifixion, and that people invented Christianity after His death. However, all the claims of Jesus when He was on earth, about Himself, about God, and about the way of salvation, contradict all the basic teachings of Islam.

This explains why serious Muslims reject the Bible and cling to the so-called *Gospel of Barnabas,* a book that betrays itself internally and historically as an Islamic forgery.

Muhammad consistently claimed that he brought no new religion or revelation other than the one Jesus brought, and Muslims claim they respect Jesus. Yet many of their actions and words establish Islam as the most anti-Christian religion on earth.

Real Islam (not nominal Islam) is more antagonistic to the Christian faith than Communism ever was. With all the persecutions Christians suffered in the former Soviet Union, (and today in China), the Church of Christ still continued, though underground. But confession of Christ by a national in an Islamic country is grounds for public execution. No church, official or otherwise, is allowed.

Islam is as political as Communism. Communism, too, is a religion, albeit, without prayer and fasting, with its own false prophets as Marx and Lenin, and its own false paradise.

America fought Communism but fails to realize that Islam is an even greater political threat with its total unification of religion and politics. Muslims realize that the teachings of Jesus Christ are far different from those of Muhammad. Thus they fear the Bible and don't want their followers to read it and discover the lies of Islam.

In September 1992, a Saudi Arabian citizen, Sidiq Mulallah, was beheaded by the Saudi government because he, as Muslim, abandoned Islam and embraced Christianity, an act of high treason and punishable by death according to Sura 4:89. Secondly, he imported a copy of the Bible into Saudi Arabia, Allah's sacred land.[2]

Sometimes, Islamic authorities of Saudi Arabia do not bother much about English Bibles since most of the citizens cannot read English. But an Arabic Bible is very dangerous. It is capable of exposing the lies of Islamic leaders and undermining their authority.

Although Jesus' teachings contradict Muhammad's Qur'an, Christ did not come to establish a religion in the real sense of the word. He brought redemption and reconciliation, bringing to those who will accept Him a Father-child relationship with God. He did not come to prescribe a uniform system of worship.

When a person is in the right relationship with God, he has the freedom to worship Him in the best way he can express himself, and not follow any mechanical movement of the body or a prescribed prayer liturgy. Religion is a man-made attempt to save oneself, while redemption is God's way of saving man. *"God was in Christ, reconciling the world unto himself"* (2 Corinthians 5:19). That is God operating, not man.

Jesus lived the life of God and imparted this life into all those who believed in Him. After His resurrection, *"...He*

2) *News Network International* (1/1/93). From U.S. State Dept. *Human Rights Report.*

breathed on them (disciples) and saith unto them, Receive ye the Holy Ghost... " (John 20:22). This is the Spirit that sealed the adoption of these disciples as children of God, and it is that Spirit that was bearing witness with their heart that they were the sons of God.

Speaking of this Spirit of adoption, the apostle Paul said, *"if any man have not the Spirit of Christ, he is none of his,"* (Romans 8:9b) —even if he has a popular religion. *"But as many as received him, to them gave he power* (privilege, opportunity, right, authority) *to become the sons of God"* (John 1:12; 2 Corinthians 1:22).

Christianity is all about possessing and living the life of Christ in the power of the Holy Spirit. It is more than religion, even in its most refined form. The Apostle Paul says:

> "For we are the circumcision, which worship God in the spirit, and rejoice in Christ Jesus, and have no confidence in <u>the flesh</u> (credentials of an outward religion, race and education).
>
> Though I might also have confidence in the flesh. If any other man thinketh that he hath whereof he might trust in the flesh, I more: Circumcised the eighth day, of the stock of Israel, of the tribe of Benjamin, an Hebrew of the Hebrews; as touching the law, a Pharisee; Concerning zeal, persecuting the church; touching the righteousness which is in the law, blameless.

> But what things were gain to me, those I counted loss for Christ. Yea doubtless, and I count all things but loss for the excellency of the knowledge of Christ Jesus my Lord: for whom I have suffered the loss of all things, and do count them but dung, that I may win Christ, And be found in him, not having mine own righteousness, which is of the law, but that which is through the faith of Christ, the righteousness which is of God by faith:
>
> That I may know him, and the power of his resurrection, and the fellowship of his sufferings, being made conformable unto his death.[3]

Here was a man you might call "the former Chief Imam of Tarsus." But he discovered that a man is not saved by human might in struggling to keep the Law. Islam is a religion of law that caters more to the outward appearance, the flesh. But Jesus came to fulfill the the Law (Matthew 5:17).

He alone was able to keep the Law, and the whole thing was finished on the Cross. Man has been unable to keep the Law. But Christ did so as "the Son of Man," and the perfect representative of Man. Therefore, when a man receives Christ into his life, God clothes him with Christ's righteousness:

> For as many of you as have been baptized into Christ have put on Christ.[4]

3) Philippians 3:3-10.
4) Galatians 3:27.

God sees Christians INSIDE Christ, and it is only inside Him that God sees us righteous. God:

> Blotting out the handwriting of ordinances that was against us, which was contrary to us, and took it out of the way, nailing it to his cross.[5]

Muhammad arrived 600 years after the finished work of Christ to raise up another set of laws (which are inferior to the Jewish Law), and forced people to accept this religion of Law. No one can reject the finished work of Christ and expect to be justified by works of laws (Romans 3:20).

Muslims have put themselves under a curse by what they have chosen. The Bible says all who rely on observing the Law are under a curse, for it is written:

> Cursed is everyone who continueth not in <u>all</u> things which are written in the Book of the Law to do them."[6]

Muslims boast about keeping the Law, but when they open the Bible to the Law in the Old Testament, they discover they are not keeping *the Law.* The Law of God in the Old Testament is more than Islamic ablution and killing one ram a year. When Muslims are confronted with Leviticus, they realize they are not keeping *the Law.*

As Christians, *"Christ hath redeemed us from the curse of the Law"* (Galatians 3:13). This is the good news called "the gospel" which Muslims reject. They do not realize that

5) Colossians 2:14.
6) Galatians 3:10; Deuteronomy 27:26.

it is pride in the sight of God to reject God's provision for us and then try to wash our noses, rinse our mouth and kill rams and be qualified to see the glory of God.

The Scripture says these regulations will all vanish, since they are based on human commands and doctrines. Such regulations appear to have some spirituality, especially their self-imposed worship, their false humility and their harsh treatment of the body, but they lack any value in restraining sensual indulgence (Colossians 2:22-23).

This explains why even with four wives, the religious man is still not fulfilled; he has to indulge in concubinage and *mutah.* There can be no fulfillment in any area of life unless one experiences the love of God in Christ.

We know of an African Muslim leader who had eight wives and yet died on top of another man's wife because of the charm the woman's husband put on her! Such dreaded anti-adultery charm, popularly known as *magun,* is common in some parts of the continent.

DOES THE NAME MATTER?

CHAPTER TEN

"And ye shall know the truth, and the truth shall make you free."[1]

UNLESS ONE wants to play syncretism,[2] which is self deception, every serious thinker will agree that truth is bigoted by nature. It is intolerant of lies.

If the Islamic Allah is not the Christian God, what happens to the Arabic, Hausa and Malay Bibles which contain the name ALLAH? Should they ignore that name and find a

1) John 8:32.
2 Syncretism is the mixture of different beliefs; the philosophy that there is truth in all religions; that everybody worships God in his own way; and all religions ultimately lead to the same God. No matter how popular this "faith" is becoming, it is a doctrine of devils (1 Timothy 4:1). It is a teaching of the spirit of the Antichrist which will be prevalent in this End Time.

different name for the Holy God of heaven and earth? Such a change may not be simple, knowing how much and how long they have believed in this "God."

In the following two chapters, we shall examine the relationship between a word and its referent. For example, when a Muslim says "Allah," who is he referring to (knowingly or ignorantly)?

When an Arab, Malay or Hausa Christian says "Allah" in prayer, is he referring to the same Allah of the Muslims? These Islamized languages had a name for God before Islam came into existence.

In one theory of linguistics known as semantics, a word means its referent, that is, the object it refers to, the object or image the word brings into our imagination. Using this theory, we may ask: Who is the object of worship in Islam?

We have no doubt that most Muslims who say "Allah" have in their mind the Creator of heaven and earth. But does that prove they are worshipping the same God as Christians? What if some ignorant people used the name "SATAN" to refer to the Creator-God. Would that make any difference?

It doesn't matter if someone sincerely believes in a wrong thing. One hundred percent sincerity does not make it right. One can indeed be sincerely wrong!

Every culture has a concept of a creator called by different names. The problem with most of them is their conception of this creator. Some even have more than one creator. They think of the creator as the chief idol, so they carve images to represent him. They make him even uglier than themselves, and feed him with local oil, ram and its blood, chicken and sometimes human beings.

According to the Scripture, people who ignore the Bible and "make" gods are under the judgment of God, whatever their culture, and whatever cosmology they hold to, whether primitive idolatry or intellectual New Age paganism:

> Because that which may be known of God is manifest in them; for God hath shewed it unto them. For the invisible things of him from the creation of the world are clearly seen, being understood by the things that are made, even his eternal power and Godhead; so that they are without excuse:
>
> Because that, when they knew God, they glorified him not as God, neither were thankful; but became vain in their imaginations, and their foolish heart was darkened. Professing themselves to be wise, they became fools, And changed the glory of the uncorruptible God into an image made like to corruptible man, and to birds, and to four-footed beasts, and creeping things.[3]

Some Christians think there is nothing behind idols. This is not true. An idol is nothing in itself but wood, clay, iron, bronze, etc. But whenever people make and worship an idol, Satan assigns demons who hover around it, influencing the lives of all who worship there. They often possess the

3) Romans 1:19-23.

priests or priestesses and sometimes speak through them to the adherents, some demanding sacrifices or foretelling their future (1 Corinthians 10:19-21).

All those dedicated to such gods are influenced for life by the spirits behind those idols, unless they are converted, and verbally renounce those idols.

Christians are often accused of being narrow in their views about the true religion. In a way, our accusers are right because the way to heaven is indeed "narrow" and "strait" (Matthew 7:13-14). The fact is, we need no further expansion of views beyond the words of our LORD.

In his attempt to find support and dismiss the Christian view about other religions, South African Muslim writer, Ahmed Deedat, quoting one of his heroes, says:

> There never was a false god nor was there ever a false religion, unless you call a child a false man.[4]

The Qur'an proves this line of reasoning to be false. In Sura 3:19 we read, "The true religion with Allah is Islam." That means there can be a true religion. If there is a true religion, then there must be some false religions.

What then is a false religion? Since the purpose of every religion is to fill man's spiritual emptiness and satisfy his craving and hunger for God, and since God is holy and man is sinful, a false religion is one that has not settled the sin question, yet promises man euphoria here or in heaven.

[4] Deedat, A. *What is His name?* Durban: Islamic Centre. p. 4.

Yusuf Ali calls these gods "false gods."[5] So contrary to Deedat and his philosopher, Ali says there are false gods.

Deedat's argument is also destroyed by Sura 16:36, which says, "…serve Allah and shun false gods."[6] Hilali and Khan's translation renders it "false deities."

Of course there can be a false god, and even a false man! Every reality can have a false impression. Anything that looks real but is not, is false or fake.

For example, no one on earth has ever seen God as He is in glory in heaven. Therefore any physical image "representing" him is false. When demons appear to people, they change their real features. A demon can be seen in different forms when appearing at different points. Any graphic picture of the devil is false because he changes physical form.

Who then worships a false god? He who worships an idol. If an idol is a false representation of God or a god, and the worshipper has never seen such a being in reality, then an idol is a false god. A doll, no matter how fine, is a false child, and a mannequin a false man.

Apart from physical images (idols), if a man imagines (conceives of) God as different from the one, true God of the Bible and worships such a "God," (no matter how sincere he may be), he is just like the one who has made a physical wrong image to represent God.

Any "God" that emerges out of such imagination is a false god. God is a revelation and not an imagination. A.W.

5) Ali, Y. *Holy Qur'an,* Appendix XIII, 1938, p. 1619.
6) Pickthall's translation.

Tozer says, "Do not try to imagine God or you will have an imaginary God."

God has revealed Himself in His Word, and in the person of Jesus Christ. See Him there; know Him there. Since there is only one God, any physical image or any imagination (i.e. an image of the mind) that is different from this one real God is a false god.

Whether a man is imagining a god or carving a physical image of a god, he is making an image. A physical idol is made like the idol in the mind of the artist. So, as a physical image can be a false god, so can a mental image be a false god.

In the Old Testament, Gideon destroyed images of a false god in Israel. In the New Testament, God does not command Christians to go from house to house destroying people's physical idols. Why? Because it is a useless exercise if the images still exist in their minds.

Africans were carried as slaves to Latin America and the Caribbean with no physical idols. But the idols in their minds eventually became physical. You see them in Northern Brazil, Haiti, New Orleans, etc.

So the Bible talks of "casting down imaginations," (i.e. destroying false ideas about God in people's minds, and presenting to them the correct idea about the Creator and the creation.) This is the primary duty of the Christian, and the particular duty of this writer.

God has called us to be involved in this end-time mass iconoclasm, casting down false gods and false paradises in people's minds. As Jock Anderson said, we insist that:

If there is a God at all, then we need not a caricature of him, but a true representation, and some means of recognizing him.[7]

THE NAME OF THE LORD

God told Moses His name was "I AM THAT I AM," the name He said He did not reveal to Abraham and other people who had served Him. *"Tell them: I AM has sent you"* (Exodus 3:14). That sounds strange.

God may not need a personal name since there are no other Gods. All the so-called Gods of the heathen are idols and are nothing more than demonic spirits whose judgment has long been settled.[8]

This is one area where the Jehovah's Witnesses are wrong. They never use any other name for God than JEHOVAH. We know that the ancient Hebrew translators of the Old Testament (the Masoretes) used the name JEHOVAH. The King James Version translators used "the LORD" or "GOD" (written in small capitals).

The name JEHOVAH was originally pronounced YAH-WEH or JAHWEH which was written without the vowels for fear of pronouncing it wrongly, thus "misusing the name of the LORD" as in the Third Commandment. In its place, the Hebrew word Elohim or Adonai were used when speaking.

God surely reveals Himself by name, but more importantly, by His divine nature, His Word and the Law. If there

---

7) Anderson, Jock, *Worship the Lord*, London: Inter Varsity Press, p. 25.
8 1 Corinthians 10:19-20; Matthew 8:29.

are many names for God, such names MUST refer to Him or they are not His names at all.

The God of heaven has been called by different names in different languages. But that has not hindered the relationship too significantly or their understanding of Him. Since God has deliberately split the human language into many tongues, He may not expect us all to use the same name for Him all over the world.

Historians like Vaqqidi said Allah was actually the chief of the 360 gods being worshipped in Arabia when Muhammad rose to prominence. Ibn Al-Kalbi gave twenty-seven names of pre-Islamic deities. From the Qur'an, we can name up to nine of these idols. The Ka'aba, housing many of these gods, has remained the temple of Allah, which Muslims revere and go to worship and kiss in Mecca during the Hajj.

It is significant that even if a Muslim is not in Mecca, he must always face toward the shrine (Ka'aba) while praying. History says pagans in Arabia were visiting Ka'aba on pilgrimage before Islam started.

Mecca was a commercial and religious center, and foreign merchants and Arabians faced the Ka'aba in prayer because that was where most of their gods were deposited. Many of the gods were brought by these merchants from their countries.

Interestingly, not many Muslims want to accept that Allah was already being worshipped at this Ka'aba shrine in Mecca by Arab pagans before Muhammad came. They do not want to accept the fact that the ways *hajj* was performed in those days by the pagan Arabs is the same as today: wearing a seamless cloth, the shaving of hair, the running around the Ka'aba shrine, the sacrifices, etc.

Some Muslims get upset when confronted with these facts. But they are proven by pre-Islamic literature. In the Qur'an, we see that pre-Islamic pagan Arabs made their strongest oaths in the name of Allah because they believed he was the most powerful of their gods (Sura 6:109). The pagans already regarded him as the creator, the lord of the shrine, the lord of Ka'aba, and the territorial god of Mecca.

Ka'aba was known as *"baithu'llah"* ("house of allah"). All other idol shrines in other regions in Arabia were also called "baithullah." Muhammad said he had been called to worship *"the god of this house"* (that is the shrine of Ka'aba).⁹"

In the Qur'an, Allah was called "the Lord of this city (Mecca)."[10] That means he was a territorial god. That is the reason for the pilgrimage, and why every Muslim *must* face towards Mecca while praying. If he faces elsewhere he knows he is not facing Allah.

Apart from Allah, other major deities being worshipped inside the Ka'aba by these pagans of Mecca were Al-lat or Allat (which is the feminine form of the word "allah"), as well as the other female idols, *al-Uzza* and *al-Manat* (Sura 53:19-20). According to al-Tabari, the *gharaniq* (female) idols were regarded as daughters of Allah.

Other popular idols were *Wadd, Suwa, Yaguth, Ya'uq,*

9) Suras 106:3; 27:91; 6:109.
10) Sura 27:91 (Yusuf Ali) plus other versions.

Nasr and *Hubal*, which Muhammad's wife, Khadijah, sacrificed to and worshipped because her sons to Muhammad were dying young.[11]

Another proof that Allah was already being worshipped as an idol in Arabia is the fact that Muhammad's father was called Abdallah or Abdullah, meaning "the servant or slave of Allah," yet he wasn't a Muslim! He was an idol worshipper, and was named after that idol.

Some have taken this to mean that Allah must be the Almighty God. But this only proves that Allah was already known in Arabia to be a supernatural being. It is NOT a proof that he is God Almighty.

Ibn Ishaq, one of the earliest biographers of Muhammad, provides one of the most authentic records on the history of Muhammad.[12] He tells how Muhammad's father, Abdu'l Muttalib, who was Muhammad's paternal grandfather, vowed to sacrifice a son to Allah if he was protected from his people who were opposing his Zamzam well project.

When he eventually succeeded in the work and also had his sons, he brought them into Ka'aba, *"stood by Hubal praying to Allah"* while lots were cast to determine which son would be sacrificed. The image of the idol Hubal was there. The lot fell on Abdullah. He was taken before two other idols, Isaf and Na'ila, for slaughtering.

Some people protested, so a further leading of an idol

11) Sura 71:23; See also the book, *The Life of Muhammad*, by Egyptian Islamic scholar, Mohammed Haykal, p. 69.
12) Guillaume, A. *The Life of Muhammad*, a translation of Ibn Ishaq's, Oxford University Press (1955) pp. 66-68.

had to be sought to determine what to do. Abdullah was then taken to "the Nijaz for there was a sorceress who had a familiar spirit" in that place.

The woman needed time to consult her familiar spirit (a demon) to know if Allah would say if the child must still be slaughtered for him. "When they had left her, Abdul Muttalib prayed to Allah, and when they visited her the next day, she said, 'Word has come to me…'" She said several camels should be sacrificed "until your lord is satisfied."

This was done and Abdullah was spared. From that time, he was dedicated to "the lord," before he grew up and gave birth to Muhammad.

In this revealing incident in the life of Muhammad's grandfather, who was "the lord"? It was Allah. What about Hubal? Pockock says the word "Hubal" could be from Ha-Baal or HuBaal in Hebrew (meaning "the lord"), a Moabite god that was imported into many nations, including Israel.[13]

On many occasions God destroyed some of the children of Israel for worshipping this god (Numbers 25:1-9). From Ibn Ishaq's account, praying to Allah was the same as praying to Hubal. As Ha-Baal or *Hu-Baal* means "the lord," so "al-ilah" or "al'lah" means "the god."

It is interesting that many Muslim leaders are afraid to research the origin of Islam, especially the pre-Islamic Arabian religion, for fear of discovering anything that will cause their faith in Islam to wane.

---

13) Nehls, Gerhard. *A Practical and Tactical Approach to Muslim Evangelism,* Life Challenge (Africa), Nairobi, 1992, p. 10.

ISLAM AND THE CRESCENT

Why does Islam regard the moon as sacred? Why are many Muslim priests astrologers? What link has the Islamic religion and Allah with the Crescent Moon and Star symbols on the minarets and domes of their mosques, and the flags of Islamic nations? What link is there between the moon and the Ramadan fast?

Professor A. Guilluame, an expert in the Islamic religion, says the worship of the moon god was rampant in Arabia at the time of Muhammad. According to him, the moon god had several names, one of which was "Allah." Recent archeological finds give the most convincing proof of the image of the chief idol of the pre-Islamic Meccans with the symbol of the crescent and the star.[14]

Middle East scholar, E.M. Wherry, in his monumental work, *A Comprehensive Commentary on the Qur'an* shows that the worship of Allah and the worship of Baal (Huba'l) involved the worship of the heavenly bodies: the moon, the stars and the sun.[15]

On the issue of Muttalib's son (Muhammad's father) bearing "Abdullah," it may be like people in Africa and Northern Brazil bearing Ṣàngólóni, Eṣùbíyi, Ifágbàmílà, Oròbíyi, etc, meaning: Ṣàngó (god of thunder)-owns-this, Begotten-of-Satan, Orò (community cult)-honours-me, Ifá (god of divination)-has-saved me, etc.

All these are names given to children from specific

14) Morey, Robert. *Islamic Invasion*, p. 211, Chick Publications, www.chick.com.
15) Wherry, E.M. - *Comprehensive Commentary on the Qur'an,* Osnabruck: Otto Zeller Verlag, 1973, p. 36.

idolatrous families, and they have no connection with God Almighty, but specific idols people revere as their gods.

Therefore, the fact that someone was called Abdallah is NOT a proof that "Allah" is the God of the Bible. It only proves that "Allah" was already known as a supernatural being before Islam started; and a supernatural being can be *any* spirit.

Since Abdallah was in the service of the Ka'aba shrine, it is much more probable that the Allah he was serving was one of the gods of the shrine. The father was "abd ul allah" (servant of Allah), while the son was "rasuli'llah" (messenger of Allah).

God told Moses: "I am the God of thy father" (Exodus 3:6). Allah also revealed himself to Muhammad as the god of his father Abdallah. So, is this god the Allah that Muhammad's father was worshipping and serving, the Allah he was dedicated to at a shrine?

It is true that Meccans persecuted Muhammad and wanted to kill him. But they were not against the worship of Allah. They already worshipped him. Allah was the god of the city. All they resisted was the undue monopoly Muhammad imposed on Allah over other gods in the shrine. That was why they threatened the new prophet's life.

Since Muhammad learned that his father was a servant of Allah, it is only logical that Allah should be the only god worshipped. There should be no other god except Allah, and Muhammad should be the Prophet (*La illaha il allah, Muhammadu rasul "llah.*) By becoming a prophet or servant of Allah, Muhammad was probably succeeding his father, whom he did not grow up to know.

When God appeared to Jacob, He told Jacob He was the God of his fathers Abraham and Isaac. When He appeared to Isaac, He introduced Himself as the God of his father Abraham. But when God appeared to Abram and asked him to leave his relatives in the idolatrous town of Ur and go to a land He was to show him, God was careful not to say He was the god of Abram's father. This was because Abram's father, Terah, was an idolater.

Abram left idolatry and lived and worshipped God in faith. He is known as the father of faith, and so could not have worshipped and kissed a stone as Muslims allege. Probably in an attempt to justify the worship of the moon, the Qur'an presents Abraham as addressing the moon and the sun as "my Lord" (Sura 6:77). Jews and Christians know that Abraham never worshipped or venerated the moon, or the black stone in Mecca.

I have often asked non-Arab Muslim friends why they go all the way to Saudi to dance and chant around a stone if they have big stones in their own country? Asian and African Muslims are told that the stones in their village are idols and should not be worshipped or offered any sacrifice; but the stone in Saudi Arabia is not an idol when worshipped, kissed and sacrificed to.

Every year, hundreds of thousands flood Mecca. Huge sums of money pour into the Saudi treasury for the pilgrimage. Many Muslims are really zealous and sincere, and some have to borrow the money for the pilgrimage, enduring all the hazards of the pilgrimage. Every year, many die. Some even go expecting to die there.

When God sent Moses to the Israelites in Egypt, He told Moses to introduce Him to them as the God of their forefathers. But God was careful to cite those forefathers... the God of Abraham, Isaac and Jacob (Exodus 3:6).

Egyptians, no doubt, had a name for the supposed Creator of heaven and earth, and the Israelites must have known this name. Moses lived in Egypt for forty years and knew all about their religion and gods.

But Moses did not claim that one of the common great gods of Egypt had revealed himself to him. He introduced another name entirely. When Moses approached Pharaoh, he did not go in the name of the chief god of Egypt. He went with the name of a different God he had encountered:

> And afterward Moses and Aaron went in,
> and told Pharaoh, "Thus saith the LORD
> God of Israel: "Let my people go, that they
> may hold a feast unto me in the wilderness."
> And Pharaoh said, "Who is the LORD
> that I should obey his voice to let Israel
> go? I know not the LORD, neither will I
> let Israel go."[16]

Pharaoh would not have dared ask such a question if Moses had appeared in the name of any of the gods of Egypt. We would be wrong, therefore, to suggest that there is nothing in a name.

16) Exodus 5:1-2.

Muhammad rose up to proclaim a message from Allah, the god of the Ka'aba shrine his father had been dedicated to. He insisted that only Allah should be worshipped. By his military prowess, he brought the Meccans to their knees. But even though all the images in the Ka'aba shrine were removed during his second pilgrimage from Medina to Mecca, all the idolatrous rituals in the shrine during pre-Islamic pilgrimages remain the same until today.

A former Muslim woman (now a Christian) told me that when she went to Mecca for the *hajj* (pilgrimage), she was appalled at the nature of the ceremonies. She refused to perform the rituals at Ka'aba and Maqam Ibrahim because she felt a strong aura of traditional idolatry she had been involved in before. She spent most of the time in her hostel pretending to be sick.

She had been told in Islam that Christians are idolaters because they give Jesus the same worship they give to God. But in her own experience of the rituals during the *hajj*, her whole religion seemed to be an organized "monotheistic idolatry" on an international scale. Her people seemed guiltier of idolatry than the Christians. From there, she learned more about the Christian faith, and eventually was converted.

We have wondered why committed Muslims never like substituting any other name for the name of Allah. So next we will examine further whether or not a certain name really matters in worship.

WHAT'S IN A NAME?

CHAPTER ELEVEN

SOMEONE MAY ASK why we have to bother ourselves with a name. What is in a name? There is a lot in a name. Proverbs 18:10 says:

> The name of the LORD is a strong tower:
> the righteous runneth into it and is safe."

How can one run into it and be safe if one does not know the name? Jesus asked Christians to baptize new believers "in the name of the Father, and of the Son, and of the Holy Spirit."

The Scripture says, "*for there is none other name… whereby we must be saved*" (Acts 4:12). Jesus says: "In my name, they (believers in Him) shall cast out devils…" Can the name of Allah be used to cast out demons?

It is also written, "That at the name of Jesus every knee

should bow."[1] Does the devil fear the name of Allah? If not, then it is not the name of the LORD that Jesus came to represent. Jesus said:

> After this manner therefore pray ye: Our
> Father which art in heaven, Hallowed be
> thy name…"[2]

The first test that Allah fails is that he is not a Father. If a Muslim says, "Our Father who is in heaven…" his own heart will rebel against it immediately. He can't continue that prayer with his heart because he does not possess the Name of the Father.

For those who contend that "Allah" is simply the Arabic translation of the name of the LORD, we say it is not so. "Allah" is more than a translation. A Christian preacher says God has many aliases. Yes, but is "Allah" one of those aliases? Is the God of the Bible the being behind the Islamic Allah? Any translation of the name of God must carry the same authority of the original name.

THE POWER IN A NAME

The Psalmist declared in adoration: "O LORD our Lord, how excellent is thy name in all the earth!"[3]

The Hebrew equivalents of JESUS are Joshua, Jeshua or Jeho-shua or Jehovah-shua, meaning, "Jehovah-saves," or "Jehovah-delivers" (Matthew 1:20-21). The Greek is *Iesous ho Christos.* The English version; Jesus Christ. The Yoruba

1) Philippians 2:10.
2) Matthew 6:9.
3) Psalm 8:1.

version; Jesu Kristi. The Ogu or Fon version; Jesu Klisti. The Hausa and Arabic translation; Yesu. All other versions referring to the same Lord carry the same weight and perform the same functions: saving and delivering from sin, sickness, Satah and evil spirits.

Other people bore the name "Jesus" during the time of our Lord. But when "Jesus Christ," or even "Jesus" is mentioned by a Christian, it refers to the Lord, and performs the same functions.

As a believer in Jesus Christ, no demon can question me as to which "Jesus" I mean if I attempt to cast it out in that name. When the sons of Sceva in Acts 19 asked some demons to come out of a mad man, the demons didn't ask "which Jesus?" The men were disgraced only because they were not Christians and had no Spirit of Christ inside them to cast out evil spirits.

Moses did not have the name JESUS. No other prophet used that name. The name God gave to Moses was "I AM THAT I AM," and Moses used that name to deliver a whole nation and disgrace the magicians and occultists of the heathen land, Egypt.

Young David told giant Goliath, "I come to you in THE NAME OF THE LORD," and he delivered a nation (1 Samuel 17:45).

If the name of Allah cannot save or deliver, what then can it do? According to those who were deep into Islam before their conversion, the name of Allah is used by Muslim occultists to make incantations, invocation and charms.

The name of our Saviour is used for good. Peter told those who arrested him and John:

> Be it known unto you all, and to all the people of Israel, that by the name of Jesus Christ of Nazareth, whom ye crucified, whom God raised from the dead, even by him doth this (former crippled) man stand here before you whole...
>
> Now when they saw the boldness of Peter and John, and perceived that they were unlearned and ignorant men, they marveled; and they took knowledge of them, that they had been with Jesus:
>
> And beholding the man which was healed standing with them, they could say nothing against it. But when they had commanded them to go aside out of the council, they conferred among themselves,
>
> Saying, What shall we do to these men? for that indeed a notable miracle hath been done by them is manifest to all them that dwell in Jerusalem: and we cannot deny it.
>
> But that it spread no further among the people, let us straitly threaten them, that they speak henceforth to no man in this name.[4]

4) Acts 4:10, 13-17.

Just like these very religious but wicked people threatening the early Christians, it seems there is something in Muslims that hates the name JESUS. Many of them, no doubt, respect Him. But when you say he is the Saviour, something rises within them in fury. Islamic hatred for Christ is almost the same universally. It is more than disagreement on doctrine.

IS "ALLAH" IN THE "ORIGINAL" BIBLE?

The vociferous South African Muslim jihadist, Ahmed Deedat, wrote a whole pamphlet[5] ridiculing the Christian God and showing that the Arabic "Allah" is in the "corrupted" Christian Bible. As if he is giving the shocker of the century, Deedat says on page three:

> It is enough, for the moment, to say that in the language of Moses, Jesus and Muhammad, the name of God Almighty is ALLAH.

What is that "shocker?" It is the presence of the Hebrew words *elohim*, *elah*, and *alah* in a footnote in an earlier edition of the Scofield Reference Bible. Deedat concludes from the footnote that these words mean the Arabic "Allah." I have seen this point repeated in at least two of his publications.

Deedat tried to convince his readers that he was a wonderful scholar of comparative religion. Much of his argument,

5) Deedat, A. *What is His Name*. This and many other books like *The God that Never Was* by Ahmed Deedat, mock the Christian concept of God, and ridicule the Deity of Christ. Yet their Qur'an warns them: "And insult not those whom they (disbelievers which includes Christians) worship besides Allah, lest they insult Allah (also) wrongfully without knowledge" (Sura 6:108).

however, falls to the ground. The words he refers to are in the footnotes and not part of the text of the Bible.

According to the editors of the same edition of the Bible, while the first two words mean "God," "alah" is a common Hebrew word meaning "to swear." Moreover, it is a verb and not a noun as Deedat thinks. The editors never suggest that those three words mean the Arabic "Allah."

Deedat knew his readers and pupils did not know Biblical Hebrew, and he is smart at riding on their ignorance by his trickery. This is the same method the Jehovah's Witnesses use to spread their heresies.

The similar-sounding word "elah" in Hebrew means an oak or terebinth. The only sense in which an oak could be associated with an attribute of God would be because it represents strength.

The word is also used as personal names for some individuals in the Bible. In Genesis 36:41, Elah is one of the dukes of Edom. In 1 Samuel 17:2,19, we have "the valley of Elah." In 1 Chronicles 4:15, Elah is one of the sons of Caleb. In 1 Chronicles 9:8, a Benjamite is also called Elah. The father of Shimei is called Elah (1 Kings 4:18); one of the kings of Israel is also called Elah. The father of Hoshea in 2 Kings 15:30 is also named Elah.

Jesus said, "Hallowed be thy name." If the LORD's Name must be hallowed, we do not expect it to be a common noun, like the name of some oak which anybody could mention any time. God commanded Israel not to take the name of the LORD their God in vain; and if we realize that Jews were afraid to even mention the covenant Name of the Lord, then we should know it would be impossible for them to give this same name or a similar one to their children.

In reference to God, the word "ela" is introduced in Ezra 4:24 and used 43 times in that book alone. It also occurs 45 times in the book of Daniel. It is significant that these two books were written by people who had been in a foreign land (Babylon or Persia) for 70 years. Although they still believed in their God, their language had been greatly influenced.

The last place this word appears in the Hebrew Bible is in Jeremiah 10:11. Jeremiah's use of the word is very significant. He used "ela" in the plural to refer to false gods:

> Thus shall ye say unto them, The gods that have not made the heavens and the earth, even they shall perish from the earth, and from under these heavens.

Every other time the word "elah" is used in the original Hebrew texts, it refers to the oak tree or terebinth. In Amos 2:9, God reminds the children of Israel of the conquests He had wrought for them:

> Yet destroyed I the Amorite before them, whose height was like the height of the cedars, and he was strong as the oaks (Hebrew plural: elahim); yet I destroyed his fruit from above, and his roots from beneath.

If "elah" were the name of God, He would not have said He destroyed the Amorites as *elah*. Isaiah 1:29 says:

> For they shall be ashamed of the oaks

(Hebrew: elahim) which ye have desired,
and ye shall be confounded for the gardens
that ye have chosen.

God's name is honorable, majestic and excellent in all the
earth (Psalm 8:1); and if *elah* were His Name or even one of
His names, he could not have used it as seen above.

It is also significant that in Isaiah 44:14 *elah* refers to a
place of idolatry where man had hewn down many "elahim"
to make a religion out of them. God actually derides man
for making a god out of elah:

Then shall it be for a man to burn: he will
take thereof, and warm himself; yea, he kind-
leth it, and baketh bread; yea, he maketh
a god, and worshippeth it; he maketh it a
graven image, and falleth down thereto.

He burneth part thereof in the fire; with part
thereof he eateth flesh; he roasteth roast,
and is satisfied: yea, he warmeth himself,
and saith, Aha, I am warm, I have seen
the fire:

And the residue thereof he maketh a god,
even his graven image: he falleth down
unto it, and worshippeth it, and prayeth
unto it, and saith, Deliver me; for thou art
my god.

They have not known nor understood:
for he hath shut their eyes, that they cannot see; and their hearts, that they can-

> not understand. And none considereth in
> his heart, neither is there knowledge nor
> understanding to say, I have burned part of
> it in the fire; yea, also I have baked bread
> upon the coals thereof; I have roasted flesh,
> and eaten it: and shall I make the residue
> thereof an abomination? shall I fall down
> to the stock of a tree?[6]

If the elah of the Hebrew Bible is the Allah of Muslims; if he is the god of the Black Stone in Mecca, the owner of the Ka'aba shrine, which pagans were worshipping in Arabia and which Muslims worship today, he surely is not the "El" and the "Jah" of the Bible.

In Hebrew, "El" refers to God, and is never used in isolation to refer to any other person, place or thing. It is usually used as an affix when used to refer to a person.

For example, there is *Elkana*: God has possessed (used in eight places), *Elnathan:* God has given, *Eltolad:* kindred of God, etc. The nearest word to "El" given to a human being is "Eli," and it means "God is high." When written differently it means "my God."

Some Muslim writer may claim that "Eli" sounds like "Allah;" but the "i" included, called *Yodh,* is not part of the word and is usually a predicator or a modal as in "Elijah" ("El is Jah" or "God is the LORD").

When Jesus cried "Eli" or "Eloi" on the cross, he was not saying "God, God," but "My God, my God." This is another

6) Isaiah 44:15-19.

area where Deedat's pamphlet misses the point.

The Hebrew word for God in Genesis 1:1 is "Elohim" not "Allah," "alah" or "elah." "Elohim" appears 32 times in Genesis chapter one alone, and 2,570 times in the Old Testament.

It is a plural word which establishes the plurality in unity of deity. This negates and destroys any identity with the Allah of the Qur'an because, grammatically, the word "Allah" does not even allow plurality.

The linguistic analysis of the Arabic "Allah" would probably take a separate Ph.D thesis in itself. In an article, David L. Johnston wrote: 1) Christians were using the word "Allah" for God before Muhammad was born, and 2) "Allah is the only Arabic word for God."[7]

Both assertions are false. The Arabic word for God, whether with small or capital "g" is "ilah," not "Allah," which was what the pre-Islamic Christians used.

The most recent edition (1996) of the English translation of the Qur'an by two professors of Arabic language, Muhammad Muhsin Khan and Muhammad Al-Hilali, and approved by the Chief Justice of Saudi Arabia, Sheikh "Abdullah bin Muhammad bin Humaid, *differentiates* between "Allah" and "*Ilah*," the general "God" in Arabic language.

They translate Sura 2:163:

> And your *Ilah* (God) is One *Ilah* (God
> — Allah), *La ilah illa Huwa* (there is none
> who has the right to be worshipped but He),

the Most Gracious, the most Merciful."

Moreover, Muhammad advised his followers to tell Christians and Jews:

> We believe in that which has been revealed
> to us and revealed to you; our *Ilah* (God)
> and your *Ilah* (God) is One (i.e. Allah),
> and to Him we have submitted (as Muslims).[8]

Note well: Muhammad uses *Ilah* to refer to the Christian God! This shows clearly that *the name of God in Arabic is Ilah*. The Allah of Muhammad is a specific being, and here Muhammad is explaining that his Allah is the same as the *Ilah* (God) of the Jews and Christians.

Therefore to say that "Allah" is the only Arabic word for God" cannot possibly be true. Muhammad proved it himself.

In their comment on Sura 16:22 and 51 in the above translation, Professors Muhsin Khan and Al-Hilali define *Ilah* as "The One who has all the right to be worshipped."

"Ilah" refers to the common universal God while "Allah" refers to the specific "god" Muhammad calls "the Lord of this city (Mecca)" (Sura 27:91). That is, the territorial god of Mecca! The Qur'an says:

> Verily, your *Ilah* (God) is indeed One (i.e.
> Allah): Lord of the heavens and of the earth,
> and all that is between them, and Lord of

---

8) Sura 29:46 (Hilali and Khan). Ialics and brackets in translation.

every point of the sun's risings."[9]

The Islamic confession of faith is: *La ilah il allah.* The true interpretation is: "No god except the god." "Allah" does not mean "God" but "the god." The word is a contraction of two words "*al*" and "*ilah*." "The god" here means the territorial god of Mecca. Muhammad said the Allah he was commanded to worship was *"the Lord of this house (Ka'aba shrine)"* (Sura 106:3).

In his days each Arabian town and village had its own god. Allah was the chief god of the territory of Mecca, and in the Qur'an, Muhammad said:

> I am commanded only that I should serve the Lord of this city, Who has made sacred…"[10]

His reference is the territorial spirit of Mecca. It was later that he began to universalize "the Lord of this city," and put on himself as many of the attributes of the Jewish God as his mind could grasp.

Historically, the god of the city of Mecca was a moon god. That is why there is the symbol of the crescent moon and the star on the minaret of all mosques. It is the symbol of Islam.

Some argue that, if a rose by any other name is still a rose and would smell as sweet, then God by any other name would still be God. That is lame logic. What about a devil with the name of Holy Michael, or Satan with the name of

9) Sura 37:4-5 (Hilali and Khan). See also Sura 38:65.
10) Sura 27:91 (Shakir).

Yehovah? Satan is still Satan even if he is clothed with some garments (attributes) of Jehovah.

A rose indeed remains a rose even if given another name. But when a wild, dangerous, colorful plant is given the name "rose," the new name does not make it a rose. That is why the Bible says Satan can disguise himself as an angel of light (2 Corinthians 11:14-15).

When Jesus told some Jews, "Ye are of your father the devil…" (John 8:44), He meant exactly what He said. Whether these particular Jews were using the name of Allah or Yahweh, their father was still the devil.

Even if Muslims use the name "Yehovah" for the god that inspired Muhammad and is working in them, their father is still different from the Father of our Lord Jesus Christ. No serious Muslim who knows Islam very well denies this.

Why did Jesus call these Jews children of Satan? Because they refused to believe the Scripture that spoke of Jesus. The problem Jesus had with these Jews was their religious spirit that opposed the plan of God for the salvation of the world. They were under the control of a power they thought was of God almighty (John 16:2).

The Jews that hated Jesus had no Scripture to support their evil attitude towards Him or Christianity. But the Muslims *do* have a sacred book, the Qur'an, that teaches them their doctrine and attitude against Christians.

That is why the Crusades could not have been a "Christian jihad." The Crusades were part of the Roman Catholic wars of expansion and not supported by scripture in any way. We do not say this because of a hatred for the Roman Catholics. It is simply history.

CONVICTION AND INTENTIONS

Partial truth presented as the whole truth is deception, and the origin of all deception is the devil. The core and key questions we should be asking are these: Was Muhammad under an inspiration of a spirit? Was he partially under the Spirit of God, and another time under another spirit?

In a write-up referred to earlier, David Johnston says:

> I don't believe anyone worships the devil
> while they are consciously worshipping God.
> He is the only one who can judge the human
> heart and discern its true intentions.

I believe that is simplistic. I have worked among idolaters and serious Muslims. I *know* (not just *believe*) that you can indeed worship the devil and believe you are worshipping God Almighty.

An "angel Gabriel" or "Michael" can appear to you and give you a message that you believe is from God. You may believe this with all sincerity but be in error. There would be no "Christian" cults without such possibilities.

Think about all those who have misled thousands or millions all over the world. Think about the victims of cult leaders who believed with all their heart they were following a minister of God.

For example, a Mormon believes with all sincerity that he is hearing the voice of God or an angel of God in the

Book of Mormon.

Jim Jones believed he was hearing from God.

Jesus told that Samaritan woman:

> Ye worship ye know not what: we know
> what we worship: for salvation is of the
> Jews."[11]

This is a profound statement. A man may worship a wrong thing with all sincerity. But the moment he knows the true identity of *what* he is worshipping, he will likely change if he is wrong. The moment an ancestral worshipper or necromancer discovers he is not worshipping or speaking to his departed ancestor but a demon, he will stop. The moment a sincere Muslim knows the true identity of *what* he is worshipping, he will stop and turn to Christ.

In Nigeria and Indonesia, most religious riots instigated by Muslims begin from the mosque, immediately after the Friday *jumat* service. Non-Muslims in Muslim dominated areas of Nigeria like Kano and Kaduna know that anything can happen on a Friday after 1:00 pm prayers. Don't these Muslims believe they are "consciously worshipping God?"

Part of the final instructions to the 9/11 hijackers says:

> If the taxi takes you to the airport, repeat
> the supplication one should recite upon rid-
> ing a vehicle … smile and be at peace with
> yourself because Allah is with the believ-
> ers and because the angels guard you even
> though you may not be aware.… You are

11) John 4:22.

> embarking upon a mission that Allah is pleased with… And if you kill, then kill completely, because that this is the way of the Chosen One (the Prophet Muhammad). …Don't take revenge for yourself only, but make your strike and everything on the basis of doing it for the sake of Allah. …And let your last word be, "There is no god except Allah, and Muhammad is His messenger."

These terrorists on the planes prayed to Allah to the very last minute. Why would young men sacrifice their lives if they did not "consciously" believe they were rendering a service and worship to God? What were their "true intentions?"

They would not do this without serious conviction. They truly believed they were fighting for God, and did not hide it. Does that conviction and intention make them right? No, they do not bring us an inch closer to God.

If one lives among Muslims as I have done for about forty years, one would need to be cautious about his verbal approach to people who have always believed the Almighty God to be Allah. You cannot say to a Muslim, "Your Allah is a demon." Even if someone is not a Muslim, he or she believes in a Creator, unless he is a fool (Psalm 14:1), and we can start from there.

After a Muslim comes to the knowledge of the truth, he will have to conclude that either there was no God revealing anything to Muhammad, or the Allah of the Qur'an is not the God that revealed Himself in the Bible. We end up

producing spiritual schizophrenics if we tell a Muslim that
the God almighty indeed sent Muhammad and that the
Bible is the Word of God.

If we say God revealed Himself progressively from the
Old Testament to the New Testament, we cannot accept the
god Muhammad presents as the same God, no matter what
they may seem to have in common.

"ALLAH" AND CHRISTIAN WORSHIP

This issue of the identity of Allah is very disturbing indeed.
How can we have the foregoing points and not develop an
aversion towards the very name? And if we do, how do we
communicate the Gospel to Arabs and those in the Middle
East without using the word?

Moreover, there are still many languages that have no
translation of the Bible, and we bother our heads about the
existing ones because of a name purported to be referring
to God.

In Malaysia, the Bible in the Malay language (called "Al-
Kitab") has been banned by the Islamic government since
1981 because it has the word "Allah" as well as some other
words that are claimed to have an Islamic origin.

It is a law in that multi-religious country, where Islam
claims 53%, that no religion other than Islam should use
certain words in its literature, including "Allah," "faith,"
"belief."

Obviously, this law was inspired by an anti-Christian
spirit in order to prevent the communication of the Gospel

to Muslims in that country.

The question becomes: is it impossible to preach the Gospel to people who have believed the Creator to be Allah without the use of that name? Should we expunge the name from such translations of the Bible and find some other descriptive names for God?

In the Arab Christian world, should we keep using the name Allah in our church services? Or do we have to reduce the Godhead to the limitation of human language? What happens to Christian Arabs who have grown believing the Supreme Being is Allah? Would there be a problem if they continued believing in Allah as the God and Father of our Lord Jesus and worship him in truth and in Spirit?

These are not simple questions. Some have even wondered whether one can worship God in truth and in Spirit in the name of Allah. Jesus said:

> "For where two or three are gathered together in my name, there am I in the midst of them."[12]

What if we gather in the names of both the Lord Jesus as well as an Allah? Whatever the case may be, there must be inseparability between a name we use for God and the name of Jesus.

It is not easy imposing an opinion on the use of "Allah" in our worship. Yet we need to realize that names matter in worship and adoration. Even idol worshippers know this.

Can we, for example, use the name Eck, the "God" in

12) Matthew 18:20.

Eckankar, in our services and say it doesn't matter? What prevents us from using Krishna, Shiva, Vishnu, Devi, Brahman —the Hindu's so-called manifestations of "the one God?"

Those who think these names can be used in Christian worship might have fallen into the snare of the Antichrist's interfaith theology that is sweeping the Western world today.

An expert in Islamics, Frans Zegers of the Netherlands, believes that one reason why the church is weak in the Arab world is the invocation of Allah in their worship services, even though they do it with all sincerity.

As I was getting disturbed by this issue, the Spirit of the Lord gave me three Scriptures. In the first, Zechariah prophesies that when Jesus comes back, He will be:

> ...king over the whole earth: in that day shall there be one LORD, and his name one.[13]

In the second Scripture, Zephaniah 3:9, God says:

> For then will I turn to the people a pure language, that they may all call upon the name of the LORD, to serve him with one consent.

From these two Scriptures, we see that the only reason for restoring a pure language is to have the correct Name of God in WORSHIP.

In the third Scripture, the Lord explains that the other

13) Zechariah 14:9.

reason He would do something about our language is:

> That he who blesseth himself in the earth
> shall bless himself in <u>the God of truth</u>; and
> he that sweareth (takes an oath) in the earth
> shall swear by <u>the God of truth</u>.[14]

In other words, there will be no more confusion or deception as to who Allah is in Islam or Christianity. There will simply be no more "Allah." Whatever the historical reality of a people, nobody must mention that name again or the name of any other god different from "the God of truth." The time will come…

> That at the name of JESUS, every knee
> should bow, of things in heaven, and things
> in earth, and things under the earth; And
> that every tongue should confess that Jesus
> Christ is Lord, to the glory of God the
> Father.[15]

The Psalmist says:

> Their sorrows shall be multiplied that hasten
> after another god: their drink offerings of
> blood will I not offer, nor take their names
> into my lips.[16]

14) Isaiah 65:16.
15) Philippians 2:10-11.
16) Psalm 16:4.

THE VISIONS OF MUHAMMAD

CHAPTER TWELVE

All the gods of the nations are idols: but
the LORD made the heavens."[1]

IF ONE WORSHIPS the chief idol of a land, what difference does it make? How is one different from the person
who worships many idols or no god at all? Veteran missionary
evangelist Dr. Lester Sumrall says:

> Muslims worship one god and we (Chris-
> tians) worship one God, but there all simi-
> larity ends. Muhammad's "god" is radically
> different from God as He is revealed to us
> by the Bible. Muhammad's god is a spiteful,
> selfish autocrat who must be placated with

1) Psalm 96:5.

> a monotonous routine of holy motions.
> The God we worship is a loving, compas-
> sionate Father who asks only that we love
> Him in return...[2]

This observation reinforces our convictions on the spirit behind Islam. But the question remains: is only one god worshipped in Islam? We cannot serve the devil and worship him ONLY. If one worships the devil in any guise, he worships him through devils. There is in reality no monotheism (or more appropriately, monolatry) in heathenism. One cannot serve Satan and not have relationship with demons.

Most operations and interactions in the occult and all Christless religions are more with these demonic spirits than with Satan himself. This is because Satan is not omnipresent. He is not God, but a fallen angel. He cannot be in all places at the same time.

We don't know why Muslims think there is anything new or wonderful in their assertion of the oneness of God. Jews also believed there is only one God. As Muslims chant their creed, "*la illaha...*," so the Jews in their synagogues chant, "*Huh echad veein sheni*," ("He is one and there is no second"); but that does not mean they were serving God when many of them rejected Jesus.

Even in the obviously polytheistic Hindu religion, we find similar confessions in the Vedas, their sacred books. Buddhists, too, believe in millions of gods, yet in many of their temples we find the inscription "Brahman is one and

2) Sumrall, Lester, *Where Was God When Pagan Religions Began?* Nashville: Thomas Nelson, p. 140.

there is no second." And Buddhism and Hinduism existed for centuries before Islam started.

What new thing is Islam proclaiming by its claim of "no other god but Allah?" Any religion can say its god is the only one existing. The Bible shows that a belief in one God is not sufficient to take a man to heaven. Man must believe in the real and true one God:

> "Thou believest that there is one God;
> thou doest well: the devils also believe,
> and tremble."[3]

So what is the big deal? Demons are also monotheists. They bring polytheism as one of their deceptions. They can deceive with polytheism, atheism, or a form of monotheism. So if Muslims worship a god other than the one and only revealed God of the Bible, they are not monotheists, whether they realize it or not.

WHERE WAS GOD WHEN ISLAM STARTED?

If Muhammad introduced a wrong god, whose fault is it? Why did the true God not reveal Himself to Muhammad and the Arabs? If He did not, will He be just to condemn Muslims on the Day of Judgment?

History records that Muhammad, after acquiring much wealth from his caravan trade, left his business in search for spiritual realities (as many people do today, getting involved in psychic practices when they get disenchanted with material things). He belonged to the *Hanifas* or "seekers of truth,"

3) James 2:19.

a group of agnostics. It was their practice to seek "light" through inner consciousness (meditation) in the ninth lunar month of the year.

Much of the Hindu religion passed through the Middle East on its way toward Europe, and left with the teachings of the techniques of detaching oneself from the world of things and ideas or "*maya.*"

After leaving his business, Muhammad spent most of his time meditating in the Cave of Hira, about three miles from the city of Mecca. During one of his meditations he was said to have been called to preach.

Who called him? And what was he commanded to preach? What he preached will help us determine whose messages he carried. Moreover, the type of meditation a person is involved in determines who can speak to him and which being(s) he can come in contact with.

WHAT MEDITATORS SAY

After his conversion to Christ, Swedish former occultist and Meditation teacher, Valter Ohman, said:

> If meditation is not thoroughly Christian,
> it leads to pagan communion with spirits.
> Meditation based on a false ideology brings
> people into contact with false spirits and a
> false god. The result is not liberation but
> oppression and possession.[4]

After giving his life to Christ, East Indian (Trinidadian)

4) Koch, Kurt, *Occult A.B.C.*, Michigan: Grand Rapids, 1980, p. 144.

Hindu yogi, Guru Rabindranath R. Maharaj, wrote in his autobiography:[5]

> I now understood that these were beings I had met in yogic trance and deep meditation, masquerading as Shiva or some other Hindu deity.

The renowned Transcendental Meditation teacher, Vale Hamilton, (who later became a born-again Christian), also describes her experiences in Meditation:

> As my consciousness extended, I became aware of the presence of spirit beings sitting on either side of me when I was meditating, and sometimes at night, they would sit on my bed. I spent three months meditating from three to ten hours a day. I had vivid experiences of demonic oppression while there. In the night during sleep, I woke with a sense of fear and apprehension as pressure was being put all over my head and body by a spirit who was trying to enter my body.... I did not consider the possibility of Satan and his demons at that time, but just accepted it as a really weird trip.... I even mistook them for guardian angels at times.[6]

Christians do meditate. But we meditate on the Word

5) The book is called *Death of a Guru* (co-authored with Dave Hunt).
6) David Haddon and Vale Hamilton, *T. M. Wants You!* Grand Rapids: Baker House, pp. 67, 73.

of God. Christian meditation must never be mistaken for the Transcendental Meditation of all Christless religions and cults.

God has given man the privilege to be in control of his mind. Christian meditation is *with* the mind, not without it. We do not try to empty our minds. The mind can never be empty. When man tries to run away from the realities of life by psychic practices, he opens his mind to demonic influence, to "the prince of the power of the air." He is no longer in control of himself. He gets "possessed."

Unless he is converted to Christ, and renounces such practices and receives total deliverance, these demonic forces will continue to influence his life until he dies.

Most occultists come in contact with what many of them call "the being of light" during their meditations, especially during their "astral travels." This "being of light" is referred to by different names in different cults. He is the "Eck" in Eckankar Movement, the "Das" or "Krishna" in Hare Krishna Consciousness. Mystical organizations like the Rosicrucian (AMORC) call him "the angel of light." Some even regard such a being as the "Grand Master Jesus" or "God!"

According to the Bible, however, these beings are that same old liar and deceiver and some of his angels assigned for that purpose:

> And no marvel, for Satan himself is trans-
> formed into an angel of light. Therefore, it
> is no great thing if his ministers (servants)
> also be transformed as the ministers of righ-

teousness; whose end shall be according to
their works.[7]

The question again is: With whom did Muhammad
come in contact during his meditations?

IS MUHAMMAD NOT A PROPHET?

Whatever their spiritual and physical manifestations,
only two spiritual forces are working in the world today,
"the Spirit of truth," and *the father of lies* (John 16:13; 8:44).
ANY spiritual experience that does not come from the Holy
Spirit is from "the father of lies."

Some still wonder if Muhammad can be regarded as a
prophet. From his history, I believe he was a prophet. What
is a prophet? The English word "prophet" has its root from
the Greek word *pro* which means "in place of," and *phemi*,
which means "speaking." It is from the former that we have
the English word "pronoun," a word used "in place of" a
noun. It is from *phemi* we have the suffix of "blasphemy"
which means "bad or irreverent speaking against God."

A prophet, therefore, is a person who speaks for, or in
place of another, especially, a god. Such a person may receive
words directly from the god or God, or sometimes he can
simply be inspired to speak or act. The prophecy could be of
past or current events (forth-telling) or foretelling of future
events. What is important is that the person is being inspired
by a power higher than himself.

From his history and the realities of Islam, one should

7) 2 Corinthians 11:14-15.

believe that Muhammad was a prophet, even a prophet of Allah. But is his Allah the God Almighty, the holy and triune God that revealed Himself to all the prophets in the Bible? Our salvation depends on our understanding of this issue.

If Allah is the real God and his words are true, and the words in the Qur'an are his words, then all Bible believing Christians are surely lost.

On the other hand, if this Allah is a demonic spirit disguised as God Almighty, then every truth-seeking Muslim must consider this matter *very* seriously.

The Scriptures say we should try the spirits behind all who claim to be prophets. But if we have a morbid fear of blasphemy, we will never try a supposed spirit of God. Such a fear has led to serious bondage and the deception of a great number of people, resulting in eternal damnation.

This is a great weapon Islamic leaders use to keep people in bondage. But every man is personally responsible to God for what he believes. God has given us a standard to judge all claims of spiritual experiences. This is why Muslims must relax and let us do the probing together.

THE NATURE OF MUHAMMAD'S VISIONS

The Arabic word "qur'an" comes from a word which means "recitation." That is why the messages in the Qur'an are regarded as the words of Allah, as dictated to Muhammad piece by piece in his visions. It is upon these visions that the faith of over 800 million Muslims hangs.

All the evidences of plagiarism of Jewish tradition and

folktales not withstanding, the Qur'an cannot be said to be only a wholesale documentation of such traditions. We do believe that Muhammad had some supernatural encounters, at least at the initial stage of his mission. We cannot explain this away because the *Hadith* includes facts of his experiences as told by those in Islam who were close to him.

If he had no such experiences, he would be a philosopher, not a prophet. It is true that he had friends who were acquainted with the Christian, Jewish and Zoroastrian religions, and he copied some of their traditions (e.g. the use of beads in prayer), yet Muhammad had some spiritual influences before he established his own religion.

According to the *Hadiths*, Muhammad had visions. Both the Shiites and Sunnishese hold these *Hadiths* as reliable. This is a crucial area, and it is important to stress that these stories were written by Muslims, not Western historians. These are the testimonies of Ibn Ishaq, Husain ibn Muhammad, Ibn Athir, Muslim, Abu Huraira, Al Bukhari, and even Zaid ibn Thabit, the Scribe of Muhammad and the traditional editor of the Standardized Qur'an.

According to these witnesses, whenever "the Inspiration" came upon Muhammad, he normally fell to the ground, with his body shaking violently, perspiring intensively, eyes shut, mouth foaming and his face looking like that of a young camel. Sometimes, he heard a bell ringing in his ears. The experience was normally followed by severe headaches. Abu Huraira says in the *Hadith:*

> ...when Inspiration descended on the
> Apostle, they used to bathe his sacred head

with henna, because of the headache that
used to come on.[8]

However, the experiences were not always so serious.
Sometimes, he simply looked as though intoxicated. Islamic
author Muhammad Haykal records that when Muhammad's
wife, Aisha, was accused of adultery, Muhammad received a
revelation "accompanied by the usual convulsion" to exoner-
ate the wife.[9]

At first, Muhammad was very sincere and suspected he
might be under the influence of a demon. How must he
have felt being strangled if it was a good God that wanted
to give a message? Must he have such serious convulsions
and fits before receiving a message from God? How are these
different from what happen in idolatrous rituals? Those were
the questions that bothered him.

His guardian-wife, Khadija, seemed to have exacerbated
the confusion. She and her cousin were the people who
influenced Muhammad at this critical moment of his life.
When Muhammad started receiving his revelations, Khadija's
cousin Waraqah ibn Nawfal was quoted as saying:

> "...O Khadija, this must be the great spirit
> that spoke to Moses. Muhammad must
> be the Prophet of this nation. Tell him he
> must be firm."[10]

8) See also G. Pfander, *Mizanul al-Haqq (The Balance of Truth)* enlarged ed.,
Austria: Light of Life, pp. 343-348. See also *Mishkat al Masabih*, Sh. M.
Ashraf (1990) pp. 1252-1257.
9) Haykal, M., p. 337.
10) Haykal, M., p. 77.

She therefore encouraged him to submit to these experiences, which they alleged must be coming from the angel Gabriel.

Khadija, said to be a member of one of the heretical Christian sects, knew something about Gabriel and felt it must have been the angel giving Muhammad his messages.

After the initial experiences, however, Muhammad became fully possessed and so convinced with the Qur'anic message that he could recite it anywhere, any time.

How did Waraqah, living in the time of Nestorian and Arian heresies, know that the spirit strangling Muhammad *must* be the same as the one who spoke to Moses? Those were the two people who contributed to the confusion of Muhammad.

Even the idolaters of Mecca suspected something must be wrong. This is one reason why they rejected his messages. They called him a *majdun*, "a poet possessed."[11]

He was also called *mashur*, someone acting or speaking as a medium of evil spirits.[12] In at least eleven places, the Qur'an defends Muhammad as not being possessed by demons. These defenses prove there were strange experiences and suspicions from the people.

Before Muhammad was born, however, the Apostle John, writing by the inspiration of the Holy Spirit, warned:

> Beloved, believe not every spirit, but try the
> spirits whether they are of God: because

11) Sura 37:35-36; 68:2; 52:28; 81:22 (A.J. Arberry).
12) Sura 44:13; 25:8; 17:47; 81:22 etc.

many false prophets are gone out into the
world.

Hereby know ye the Spirit of God: Every
spirit that confesseth that Jesus Christ is
come in the flesh is of God: And every
spirit that confesseth not that Jesus Christ
is come in the flesh is not from God: and
this is that spirit of antichrist, whereof ye
have heard that it should come...[13]

Muhammed Marmaduke Pickthall, in the Introduction
to his translation of the Qur'an, says "Khadija tried the
spirit." We ask: By what criteria did Khadija try the spirit
behind Muhammad?

When the Apostle John said people should "try every
spirit," he was talking to those who knew the truth, and were
already in the light and had the standard for such trying and
judging. But Khadija, as we have learned from Muslim historians, was a regular client of the idol priests in Mecca.

When her sons were dying, she consulted idols for
divination and made sacrifices to them. How could such
a person "try" the spirit influencing Muhammad to know
its origin?

Waraqah, who joined Khadija to encourage Muhammad,
did not live to see how "the great spirit" of Muhammad denied
the deity of Christ. He died before Islam really took shape.
The Arabian "Christians"[14] at the time of Muhammad had

13) 1 John 4:1-3.
14) People and movements labeled "Christian" in this book are usually
referring to a ritualistic religion with roots in Catholicism.

no discernment of spirits because of their heresies and lack of true witness to Christ.

They had not recovered from their apostasy when Islam engulfed the whole land like a wildfire and everybody was subjugated. The "Christians" were either converted to Islam or wiped out from the Arabian Peninsula. The same tragedy looms over the Western world if true Christians do not wake up to their responsibility of drawing Muslims to Christ.

The nature of the visions and inspiration of Muhammad is perhaps the most disturbing in the history of Islam. Many writers deliberately remain silent about it to avoid any "unpalatable" interpretation; and modern Muslim scholars particularly, avoid it because of the implication, even though it is in their *Hadith*. It is dangerous for a Muslim to ignore this area.

As Christians, we cannot shrink from citing any event in history to bring out a spiritual truth, especially if such events affect us. It is the origin that matters, especially, in spiritual things. We cannot improve a thing that had a wrong beginning.

That is why Jesus told Nicodemus, *"Ye must be born again."* He must begin from zero. The problem with Islam is more than the teachings; the very source of the inspiration of the teachings is the real problem.

The faith of the Muslim is firmly based on the belief that Muhammad had a vision and visions from Allah and recited word for word what Allah asked him to say. It is that faith that makes Islam. "Islam," to them, means "submission to the will and words of Allah." Remove that belief and there is nothing called Islam.

If, therefore, we are content with the volumes on the doctrines and do not examine the source of those doctrines, we miss the whole point. This can be dangerous because we give the impression that nothing is wrong in Islam except the violence and certain doctrines.

If we take such a stand, we are not helping those sincere Muslims would be ready to change if they knew the truth. We give them the impression that we are serving the same God with differences only in our worship systems and points of emphasis. Such a stand is delusive.

Our aim, therefore, is not to urge the Muslim to try and improve his character and turn over a new leaf or start a new sect of Islam. The problem is not with the leaf or the fruit, but with the tree itself; the very seed was a wrong seed (Matthew 12:33).

The problem with Islam is more than the doctrines; it is the inspirer of the basic doctrines; it is the very god whose spirit possessed Muhammad that has the big question mark.

But whoever the Allah was that spoke to Muhammad at Hira, the true God still had a way of reaching out to him. First, Khadija and Waraqah, though they did not have good Christian testimonies, had a "Christian" background, and must have informed Muhammad more on the stories of the Bible after his initial experiences. Secondly, he had trade contacts with many Christians and Jews and learned some things about the Bible and the Christian faith through them.

Moreover, when Khadija died, Muhammad married several other wives, some of whom would have influenced his spiritual understanding if he wanted to learn about the Gospel. One of his early wives was a Jewess called Raihana. His ninth wife, Safiyya, was also a Jewess whom he had captured after killing her husband in his battle against the Khaibar Jews.

The governor of Egypt, Moqawqa, presented to him two Ethiopian Christian slave ladies, Maryam and her sister Sirin. He took the senior sister as wife. So in his household alone, Muhammad had two Christian and two Jewish witnesses. While the Jews would explain the Old Covenant of God with Israel, the two Christians could have explained the New Testament stories to him.

Muhammad could have used these opportunities to learn about Christianity. But instead of establishing his faith on the gospel stories, he collected the stories in bits and shreds, mixed them with the ones he heard during his caravan journeys, got inspired by a certain spirit, then concocted his own fictions to build his new religion.[15]

The devil has always been busy roaming about seeking whom he may use to oppose the Gospel of Christ. It seems he saw in Muhammad all he needed to exterminate Christianity, which at that time had become weak.

15) For more information on the Christian and Jewish influences on Muhammad, see *Anatomy of the Qur'an* by this author.

Moreover, because there were many Christians in the then Yathrib (which he changed later to Medina or "city of refuge" after conquering the city), Muhammad and the people of Arabia had opportunities to receive the gospel.

GOD'S LOVE FOR THE ARABIANS

No genuine Christian should have any animosity against Arabs or Muslims of any race. We must love them and demonstrate that God loves them. It was not by accident that Christians were in Arabia before the time of Muhammad. It was a perfect plan of God.

First, God had to make sure that every nation "under heaven" was represented on that glorious Pentecost morning in Jerusalem when the Church of Christ was launched or empowered. It was impossible for a handful of disciples to go to all the world to spread the gospel with no modern means of communication and transportation.

Jews were already scattered among all the nations. God used them by bringing many of them, as well as those they had converted to Judaism, to Jerusalem as representatives from all these nations.

There, on the day of Pentecost, they witnessed the launching and empowerment of the Church of Christ. They received the gospel in its freshness and went back into <u>all</u> the world and preached the gospel to every creature.

The Bible says Arabians were there on that occasion.[16] The first people the Bible mentions there are "Parthians and

16) Acts 2:11.

Medes and Elamites" (Acts 2:9). They were in the present Iran (home of Shi'ite Islam), the second "holy land" of Islam after Saudi Arabia. They were among several thousand who heard about the wonderful works of God, each "in his own language."

When Peter preached the gospel, the Arabs and Iranians among the congregation that believed, were baptized, and were immediately promised *the same gift* of the Holy Spirit that the disciples received that day (verse 38).

All these people went back home, and we can be sure that the Arabs among them began to spread the gospel in their own land in that very first century. So we can say the Gospel reached the Arabs and Persians (Iranians) in the First Century AD —over 500 years before Muhammad was born.

Moreover, when the Roman persecution started and Jews were expelled from Rome, some of them, including the Christians among them, fled to the Arabian Peninsula to continue their faith.

But many Arabs rejected the gospel and maintained their numerous gods until Allah (said to be one of the many), emerged to monopolize the scene under the human instrumentality of an energetic Muhammad with a promise to *"…fill hell with the jinn and mankind together."*[17] From there, the struggle began:

> Because that, when they knew God, they glorified him not as God, neither were thankful; but became vain in their imagina-

17) Sura 11:119 (Pickthall).

> tions, and their foolish heart was darkened...
> who changed the truth of God into a lie,
> and worshipped and served the creature
> more than the Creator, who is blessed for
> ever. Amen.
>
> And even as they did not like to retain God
> in their knowledge, God gave them over to
> a reprobate mind, to do those things which
> are not convenient; Being filled with all
> unrighteousness, fornication, wickedness,
> covetousness, maliciousness; full of envy,
> murder, debate, deceit, malignity..."[18]

At this point, an honest Muslim should be able to pray this prayer in the Qur'an:

> Our Lord! We have wronged our own
> souls: If thou forgive us not and bestow
> not upon us Thy Mercy, we shall certainly
> be lost...[19]

The Bible says, "*How can we escape if we neglect so great salvation*" offered by Christ Jesus? (Hebrews 2:3).

It is pathetic that, having led Muhammad astray and having fed him with enough gall of hatred for anything Gospel, Allah instructed Muhammad to tell his followers that he did not know what would become of him or his followers after death (Sura 46:9).

Muhammad was not sure if even he would reach the

---

18) Romans 1:21, 25, 28-29.
19) Sura 7:23 (Yusuf Ali).

paradise of wine and the sensual heaven he was preaching about. The Lord Jesus simply asks:

> Can the blind lead the blind? shall they not both fall into the ditch?[20]

So Islam is a perfect example of a religion without a redemption. And crowds of people, even respectable people, still follow! The Bible speaks of *"a broad way that leadeth to destruction!"*

> There is a way that seemeth right unto a man, but the end thereof are the ways of death."[21]

Abu Huraira said:

> "The prophet summoned Quraish (his tribesmen), and when they had gathered, he addressed them in general and in particular, saying: "B. Ba'b b. Lu'ayy, deliver yourselves from hell; B. "Abd Shams, deliver yourselves from hell; B. "Abd al-Muttalib, deliver yourselves from hell; Fatima, (my daughter) deliver yourselves from hell; for I have nothing which can avail you against Allah's punishment..."[22]

This report is also recorded in *Al-Bukhari*.

We ask: How can a man deliver himself from hell? If Muhammad told the closest people to him (and therefore the

20) Luke 6:39.
21) Proverbs 14:12.
22) In *Mishkat al Masabih*, p. 118.

most devoted), "I have nothing which can avail you against Allah's punishment," what is the purpose of his religion? Consider this if you are a Muslim.

On page 525 of the *Hadith* Mishkat, we read:

> A'isha [Muhammad's wife] said that God's messenger used to say, "O God, I seek refuge in Thee from the evil of what I have done...

On page 529 of the same *Hadith*, another witness, Abu Musa al-Ashari, quoted Muhammad again as saying:

> O God, forgive me *my sin, my ignorance*, my extravagance in my affairs and my frivolous sins, for I am guilty of all that; O God, forgive me my former and my latter sins, *what I have kept secret* and what I have done openly.

What did he keep secret? Could it be the truths and discoveries about Jesus which he refused to tell the people? All we know is that Muhammad ignored God's salvation through Jesus Christ and established his own kind of righteousness which obviously was not able to cover his own sins, much less those of his followers.

Now, fourteen hundred years have gone by and the souls of billions of well-meaning people have followed his religion and have passed away into eternity *"without a hope, without God in this world."* I am terrified to imagine that number.

Today, millions zealously follow this religion and are ready to die to defend it. At least ten million Muslims are in the United States and greater numbers in Western Europe. If Christians really love them, they will do all they can to share the Gospel of Christ with them.

Imagine if Muhammad, with his strong personality and wisdom, had been converted to Biblical Christianity. The Arab world could have been different. There might not have been the torrents of tears we had on September 11, 2001. Negligence can be costly.

Muhammad probably had good intentions at the beginning, and desired to serve the true God. But he missed it somewhere along the line because he never trusted Jesus Christ, *the Way, the Truth and the Life.*

If we Christians think deep, we will realize how precious a soul is either in the hand of God or in the hand of the devil. If we refuse to warn a sinner who is by our side and whose soul is hungry for God, do we know how far the devil can go with that soul if he fully possesses him? Men must be converted and be possessed with the Holy Spirit or else they will be diverted and…

The whole work of the devil is to get as many people as possible to be with him in the lake of fire. In the Qur'an, Allah (whoever he is), says, *"Verily I shall fill hell with the jinn (demons) and mankind together."*[23]

Dear Muslim, do not lose hope. There is a better way:

> For GOD (of the Bible) so LOVED the world (mankind), that he gave his only begotten Son, that whosoever believeth in

23) Sura 11:119 (Pickthall). Reaffirmed in Suras 7:177-178 and 32:13

him <u>should not</u> perish (in hell), but have
everlasting life (in the real heaven).[24]

Even though Allah surely will lead all those who follow
him to hell fire as he has promised in the Qur'an, if any
Muslim repents, regardless of his position in Islam, Jesus will
become the LORD of his life and he or she can become one
of His sheep. As the Good Shepherd, Jesus said:

> My sheep hear my voice, and I know them,
> and they follow me: And I give unto them
> eternal life; and they shall never perish, nei-
> ther shall any man (no devil, no strange god)
> pluck them out of my hand. My Father,
> which gave them me, is greater than all;
> and no man is *able to pluck them out of my
> Father's hand.*[25]

This is the kind of Saviour we have in Christianity. The
area a Muslim may find extremely difficult to believe in the
Bible, especially concerning the deity of Christ, is the very
place where his salvation lies. Veteran missionary evangelist
Lester Sumrall of blessed memory wrote:

> "It is just as pagan to worship the wrong
> god as it is to worship no god or to worship
> a whole pantheon of gods."

JESUS LOVES YOU!

24) John 3:16.
25) John 10:27-29.

LETTERS FROM OUR MAILBOX

Muslim wife, husband and father saved

My husband was away on pilgrimage to Mecca when I read your book on Allah and got converted from Islam to Christ. When he returned I told him the joy of salvation, but he said he would soon scatter this fundamentalist nonsense from my head. He brought home Islamic pamphlets from Ahmed Deedat to disprove the Bible. He forbade me from going to church.

My father (a very respectable Muslim) disowned me. I felt such rejection would be too much for me to bear. Then I became pregnant. There were complications, and the miracle of my delivery impressed my husband about my God, and he got converted, and renounced the "Alhajj" title he had acquired for having made a pilgrim to Mecca.

My father became terribly ill. Things were very hard at that time in our country. Nobody had money for his treatment. But God blessed me and as a banker, I had access to my money. We were the ones who took care of my dad throughout his illness.

My father then called and said my husband and I had greatly impressed him with our love and care for him during his sickness. He asked us to pray for him to be saved from his sins. He accepted the Lord, and then died.

—Mrs. Fatima, M.O.

Fulani Teacher Saved

I am a Fulani man, and a teacher. I was teaching Islamic religion; but after reading your book on Allah, I noticed some changes taking place in my life. I found it difficult to teach Islam again. Now I teach Hausa language instead...

—A. T.

"Jesus Ministered to Me"

I was a Muslim, and I must say, a fanatical one, learned in the Qur'an. During my compulsory one year voluntary service to the nation after graduation from the university, I came under serious demonic torments, especially in my dreams. Sometimes, I would be pursued by masquerades and have affairs with unknown people in the dream. Some Christians introduced me to Christian literature, of which I was very skeptical. But later I read your book on Allah, after which Jesus appeared to me in a dream. When I woke up, I got on my knees and accepted Jesus as my personal Lord and Saviour.

—A. Shakir

For more testimonies, see the book, *How We Found Jesus: 20 Ex-Muslims Testify* (edited by G.J.O. Moshay).

DECISION

If you want God to save you from your sin, and know it with the assurance of the Spirit of God in your heart, you need to pray in your own words a sincere prayer like this:

> O Lord Jesus, I know I need help. My heart convinces me if I die the way I am, I have no assurance of eternal life. I want you to save me today. I believe what the Bible says about You. I believe You are the Saviour.
>
> I invite You to come into my heart now. I believe You died for my sin, rose from the dead and are alive today in heaven. I believe You are coming again to judge the world. Lord, accept me and forgive my past.
>
> Lord Jesus, I want to begin a new life in You today. Help me to stand when trial comes to test this serious decision I am making today. Uphold me with Your mighty hand. Let not my enemies prevail over me. From now, lead me by Your Spirit. Thank you, because I believe You have heard me. Amen.

BIBLIOGRAPHY

- Abd Al-Masih, *Islam Under the Magnifying Glass*, Austria: Light of Life.

- Al-Hilali, Muhammad T., & Muhsi Khan, M. (eds), *Holy Qur'an: Explanatory English Translation*, Turkey: Hilali Publications.

- Ali, A. Yusuf, *The Qur'an: Text, Translation and Commentary,* Beirut: 1938.

- Arberry, A.J., *The Koran Interpreted*, New York: Macmillan, 1964.

- Bryant, T. Alton (ed), *The New Compact Bible Dictionary*, Michigan: Zondervan, 1967.

- Butrus, Z., *God is One in the Holy Trinity*, Rikon (Switzerland): The Good Way, PO Box 66, CH.8486.

- *Kaduna Religious Riot '87: A Catalogue of Events,* CAN Kaduna Publicity Committee, 1987.

- Christy, J.W., *Introducing Islam,* New York: Friendship Press.

- Cragg, K., *The Call of the Minaret,* Ibadan: Daystar Press 1988.

- Dawood, J., *The Qur'an: Translation*, New York: Penguin Books.

- Deedat, Ahmed, *Is the Bible God's Word?* Durban: Islamic Propagation Centre.

- Deedat, Ahmed, *What is His Name?*

- Fry, G., & King, R..., *Islam: A Survey of the Muslim Faith*, Michigan: Baker Books House, 1982.

- Gatje, Helmut, *The Qur'an and Its Exegesis*, London: Routledge and Kregan Paul, 1976.

- Gibb, H.A.R, & J.H. Kramers, *Shorter Encyclopedia of Islam*, Ithaca, New York: Cornell Univ. Press, 1953.

- Gilchrist, John. Evidences for the Collection of the Qur'an. Benoni: Jesus to the Muslims, 1984.

- Grunebaum, G.E., *Medieval Islam*, Univ. of Chicago Press, 1978.

- Guillaume, A., *The Life of Muhammad*, London: O.U.P.

- Hamid, Abdullah bin Muhammad, *The Call to Jihad: Striving for Allah's Cause*, Lagos: Ibrash Islamic Publ. Ltd., 1989.

- Hanua, M., *The True Path: Seven Muslims Make Their Greatest Discovery,* Colorado: International Doorways Publishers, 1975.

- Hoballah, Mahmoud, *Muhammad the Prophet,* Washington D.C.: The Islamic Centre.

- Holt, Lamton, Lewis (eds), *The Cambridge History of Islam* (4 vols), Cambridge: University Press, 1978.

- Jadeed, Iskander, *The Person of Christ in the Gospel and the Koran* (parts 1-2), Rikon: The Good Way.

- Jeffery, A., *Islam: Muhammd and His Religion*, Indianapolis: Bobs-Merrill, 1958.

- Khan, Muhsin Muhammad (ed), *Al Bukhari,* Lahore: Nazi Publications, 121, Fulqarnain Chambers, Granpat Rd., Lahore, Pakistan, 6th Ed., 1986 Selected portions of this Hadith repro duced in Muhsin Khan et al's English translation of the Qur'an.

- Laffin, John, *The Dagger of Islam*, London: Sphere Books, 1979.

- Lamb, David, *The Arabs,* New York: Random House, 1987.

- Lings, M., *Muhammad: His Life, Based on the Earliest Sources*, London: Islamic Texts Society, 1983.

- Marsh, Charles, *The Challenge of Islam* (formerly Too Hard for God?), London: Scripture Union.

- Morey, Robert, *The Islamic Invasion,* Oregon: Harvest House, 1992.

- Nehls, Gerhard, *Destination Unknown,* Nairobi: Life Challenge (Africa), PO Box 50770, Nairobi, Kenya.

- Pickthall, Muhammad M., *The Meaning of the Glorious Koran*, Lagos: Islamic Publications Bureau.

- *Prayers of the Prophet* (with Arabic Text, compiled and translated by A.H. Farid), Lahore: Sh. Muhammad Ashraf Publ.

- Robson, James, *Mishkat al Masabih,* Lahore: Sh. Muhammad Ashraf Publ., 1975 & 1990. Originally by Imam Hussain al-Baghawi, Lahore: The Book House.

- Siddiqt, Abdul Hadid, *Sahih Muslim,* Lahore: Sh. Muhammad Ashraf Publ., Pakistan, 1987.

- Shorrosh, Anis, *Islam Revealed: A Christian Arab's View of Islam,* Nashville: Thomas Nelson, 1988.

- Sumrall, Lester, *Where Was God When Pagan Religions Began?,* Nashville: Thomas Nelson.

- Thomas, R.W., *Islam: Aspects and Prospects,* Villach (Austria): Light of Life, P.O. Box 13, A-9503.